Seven Minutes from Home

PERSONAL/PUBLIC SCHOLARSHIP

Volume 1

Series Editor

Patricia Leavy
USA

Editorial Board

Scope

The *Personal/Public Scholarship* book series values: (1) public scholarship (scholarship that is accessible to academic and popular audiences), and (2) interconnections between the personal and public in all areas of cultural, social, economic and political life. We publish textbooks, monographs and anthologies (original material only).

Please consult www.patricialeavy.com for submission requirements (click the book series tab).

Seven Minutes from Home

An American Daughter's Story

Laurel Richardson

SENSE PUBLISHERS
ROTTERDAM/BOSTON/TAIPEI

A C.I.P. record for this book is available from the Library of Congress.

ISBN: 978-94-6300-541-8 (paperback)
ISBN: 978-94-6300-542-5 (hardback)
ISBN: 978-94-6300-543-2 (e-book)

Published by: Sense Publishers,
P.O. Box 21858,
3001 AW Rotterdam,
The Netherlands
https://www.sensepublishers.com/

All chapters in this book have undergone peer review.

Cover photo by Laurel Richardson

Printed on acid-free paper

PRAISE FOR
SEVEN MINUTES FROM HOME

"A tour de force, the penultimate statement from gifted writer Laurel Richardson. For the last three decades Richardson has defined and then charted the murky waters of critical, literary autoethnographic discourse. Here an American daughter's story comes home. We all need a starting place, seven minutes from home is a good place to begin."
– Norman Denzin, University of Illinois at Urbana-Champaign

"Laurel's *Seven Minutes from Home* takes us into her neighborhood and the mundane and not-so-mundane moments of her everyday life. We accompany her walking her beloved dogs, socializing with neighbors, eating with family, restoring her home, buying ice cream, and participating in local poetry groups. We come to know her and her neighborhood through her blending of ethnographic sensibilities and literary writing, where the past and present connect and the self is contextualized in relationships, neighborhoods, and the larger community. The stories are riveting; you will not be able to stop reading. You will identify with her experiences and they will stay with you, meaning you now will see things in your neighborhood you have not seen before and think of your identity and home in more nuanced ways than you ever thought possible."
– Carolyn Ellis, University of South Florida

"Laurel Richardson's new book *Seven Minutes from Home: An American Daughter's Story* shows what polished and accomplished contemporary research writing looks like. This book provides even more evidence about how the personal intersects with the sociological. Perhaps I should have waited a little longer to finish working on *Permission: The International Interdisciplinary Impact of Laurel Richardson's Work* (Sense, 2016)? Who knows? It is fantastic to see yet another totally new contribution to her already diverse and impressive body of work. Laurel's book certainly confirms my investigation of her profound impact on the scholarly work of so many others."
– Julie White, The Victoria Institute, Australia

"Why seven minutes from home? Because so much of life is lived within the radius of a seven-minute walk, bike or drive from home – shopping, walking the dog, going to the library, school, church or synagogue. In this vivid memoir, Laurel Richardson combines sociological insights with a feminist focus on lived-experience to bring our attention to the joy, pain and discomforts of everyday life in details large and small. A trip to the local Dairy Queen is an occasion to celebrate the diversity of patrons who share her guilty pleasure which is later tempered by the discovery of a heroin bust in that very same location. Her love of family, friends and community are captured in the routine activities of the annual neighborhood pot-lucks, monthly meals with her extended family and the annual Independence Day parade. She weaves the present with the past, helping herself and the reader cope with the inevitable changes of life like aging, illness and death. We are nourished along the way by her delicious description of her mother's recipe for chicken soup and by her enduring love of poetry. We learn about Laurel, but we also discover much about ourselves. The fabric of life she stitches together she calls 'family,' and I am glad to be a part of it. Highly recommended for courses in sociology, women's studies and creative writing."
– **Mary Margaret Fonow, Arizona State University**

"A writer is always on the lookout for worthy writers to read and learn from. Laurel Richardson is one of those writers – a respected scholar who conveys her thoughts and knowledge with a poet's voice. There's much for writers to admire and learn from her work: her lyricism, lexicon, creative structures, wide audience appeal and her ability to examine everyday events in the context of the broader world."
– **Susan Knox, essayist, fiction-writer and author of *Financial Basics***

"Laurel Richardson's sensitive memoir, *Seven Minutes from Home*, has the capacity to awaken in all of us those connections to the past that inform our present, everyday lives. Her story inspires us to see the nuanced history we bring with us and gives us permission to become empowered by it, as she has."
– **Pat Snyder, personal coach and *ThisWeek* columnist of *Balancing Acts***

"Laurel Richardson has already long established herself as a foundational scholar in many fields: sociology, autoethnography, gender studies, qualitative research. Her latest book however – *Seven Minutes from Home: An American Daughter's Story* – repositions her as something more – an elder of our scholarly community chronicling the aging but beautiful face of American life, still alive and well in Richardson's own little Ohio corner of it. This stunning little book sets itself up as a kind of *Our Town* for the 21st century, detailing as Thornton Wilder did not only the narrator's life but the lives of her neighbors and family members too. Writing in sparse but evocative prose in the style of May Sarton, Carson McCullers, and Saul Bellow (whose epigraph opens this text), Richardson invites us along her free-wheeling walk down memory lane (and around the streets of her neighborhood) not mapped by linearity or geography, but rather by associative memory, despite its mostly linear table of contents and exhortation to pay attention to *location, location, location!* The voice that narrates *Seven Minutes from Home* is still unmistakeably that of a sociologist, calling upon the traditions and forms of sociology throughout, exploring and linking time, place, action and subjectivity. I read it in one sitting on a Sunday afternoon and it made me feel homesick no end, but also deeply grateful. This is the story of a life situated within a pulsing American culture; a true melting pot full of oppression and opportunity, full of tragedy and triumph, as vibrant today as it ever was. Her brother called this book 'Americana'; I call it a love letter to a culture and a life well-lived."
– Anne Harris, Monash University, Australia

"Oddly gripping. By which I mean, I didn't expect to be pulled into it with such force from the first page. Laurel Richardson has stepped into the river of her life and has managed to face both directions. While she stands, the reader moves all around her: there is both placidity and rapid motion (rivers also have moods) and at times a kind of vertigo in the unexpected experience. *Seven Minutes from Home* takes us everywhere and anytime with revealing insight."
– Doug Storm, author of *The Gulf of Folly* and Producer and Host of the arts & culture radio program, *Interchange*, in Bloomington, IN

In Memoriam

Jessica Richardson
1928–2007
&
Barrie Richardson
1934–2015

Everything teaches transition. We dive & reappear in new places.

– Ralph Waldo Emerson

TABLE OF CONTENTS

ACKNOWLEDGMENTS

An earlier version of "Our Small World" appeared in *Culture Studies Critical Methodologies*: 2002: 24–26. Some parts of "Kisses in the Dark" appeared in *After a Fall* (Left Coast Press, 2013), and some of "Heavy Metal" has been adapted from "Alice in Computerland" in Michael Hvild Jacobsen et al. (Eds.), *Imaginative Methodologies in the Social Sciences—Creativity, Poetics, and Rhetoric in Social Research* (Farnham: Ashgate, 2014). I appreciate the republishing herein.

ROOTS

…they get certain roots and kindle them…

– The Babylonian Talmud

A glowing ember is easily rekindled.

– Irish proverb

CHICAGO BORN

I am an American, Chicago born…

– Saul Bellow

"*Location. Location. Location.* Only three words matter when choosing where to live." Or so said my criminal-attorney father. He chose Chicago, Miami Beach and, then, the beautiful and safe Key Biscayne where, in 1972, in his very own condo, he was murdered. But this book is not about his times and places; it's about mine. It is not about *him*. It is about *me*. It is neither autobiography nor memoir. Rather, *Seven Minutes from Home* is an autoethnography of my changing self in a changing society.

My body ages. Built environments are unbuilt and rebuilt. Cultural practices rise and fall. Through all those changes, though, there remains an overarching constant: I am living an American Story. Not *the* American story but one similar to other American stories in contours: differing in particulars. I am a daughter of a complexly mixed marriage. On my mother's side, I am a first-generation American. Father's mother was a Daughter of the American Revolution.

Mother's Russian-Jewish family came to America in 1908 from a stetl outside Kiev. They were escaping the pogroms. My mother was eight, old enough to remember the horrors and young enough to imagine a happier life. Gramma never learned English.

Father could trace his heritage, so he said, back to the Eleventh Century when Tyrrell the Red, a Viking, hacked out a kingdom for himself near Dublin. By the Seventeenth Century, that land was controlled by Sir Richard Tyrrell, an Irish-Catholic. One of his stead had joined the Guy Fawkes "gunpowder plot" to blow up the English parliament house. Its failure required a Tyrrell to change his location to America. From then on, Father's male ancestors in America have devoted themselves to "law-and-order."

Mother lived in a Chicago ghetto with her family. They celebrated the Jewish High Holidays with relatives who had also escaped the pogroms. At thirteen, having completed grade school, she went to work at Montgomery Ward's as a bookkeeper. I have a photo of her—an olive-skinned unmarried young woman in a black bathing suit brushing her long straight black hair. She is exotically beautiful.

Father lived in Chicago's tony north side until his parents separated when he was thirteen. His even tonier Aunt Laura, a Christian Scientist, took over his upbringing. I have two of his over-stuffed photo albums. In the high-school album, he is a handsome fair-skinned fellow in flannel pants and dress shirts, usually pictured next to a pretty young girl in a ruffled dress on a front-yard swing. In his Cavalry album, he looks jaunty training horses, palling around with the guys and schmoozing with pretty girls, their knees exposed. Mother hated that album.

After the Cavalry, Father came back to Chicago and started law school. He met Mike, my mother's communist brother, in Bug-House Square, a site of free speech in Chicago. Mike invited my father to board at Gramma's house. He was the first Gentile to ever enter her house.

When my mother and father fell in love and decided to marry, Gramma had a nervous breakdown. She recovered when my father promised that the children would be raised Jewish. Mother about had her own nervous breakdown, then, because she wanted her children safe, not Jewish. To appease everyone, my older sister, Jessica, my older brother, Barrie and I went to Anshe Emet Synagogue during the school year and to Protestant Family Camp during the summer.

Coming out of the depths of the depression in the late 1930's, my mother's family moved in with my family in our "mansion" on Lake Park Avenue on Chicago's south side. I spent the first three years of my life in that house in a bi-lingual, bi-cultural, three-generation family in a neighborhood that was becoming bi-racial. Our mansion passed onto Muddy Waters, the undisputed father of modern Chicago Blues. An historical site sign marks the house.

It was in that Lake Park Avenue house that I bodily experienced the economic, demographic and attitudinal changes of pre-World War II America. These changes were not abstractions to my pre-school self but deeply, personally felt. I had no vocabulary to understand what was happening to me, my family, my neighborhood and no words to gloss over my feelings of irreparable loss when my immediate family separated from my grandparents and moved to the north side. It was here, in Chicago, that I first lived through the internexus of public and private lives.

* * *

I am a late-in-life daughter born into a sociologically unorthodox family—parents from different backgrounds, heritages, social-classes, religions, education, and longevity of citizenship. Mother wanted to live the storybook American Dream. Father wanted to be the archetypical rogue hero: save the underdog.

The living arrangements and the match between my mother and father, if not perfect for them, were perfect for me. I learned that there are different ways to serve corned beef, live a life, tell a story. I have choices. As my brother Barrie was fond of saying, "Only in America…"

* * *

When I was fifteen, I asked permission from my parents to apply to the University of Chicago's "Hutchins Early College" program. I had read about it in the Tribune. I asked them to promise that if I passed the test and got a scholarship, they would allow me to go. My parents rarely made promises and always kept them. Although I would not have acknowledged it back then, I was ready to leave home. My father was mostly absent, my mother mostly depressed, my sister Jessica married, my brother Barrie soon to leave for college. Instead, I mouthed the cultural story that high school was boring. When I passed the entrance exam, Mother was furious with Father. Why didn't he tell her that I would pass? I matriculated.

Father was a Republican who ran for political offices and ran campaigns, such as Senator Dirksen's. He must have suffered ridicule for letting his daughter go to "that commie-red school," the U of C. But Father was also a member of the American Civil Liberties Union. He was always for the "underdog." He had faith in me.

While at the U of C, I sat in at Walgreens to help integrate the drugstore's counter; I chained myself to Frank Lloyd Wright's Robie House to keep it from being razed; I canvassed Hyde Park with partners of different races to research who would be denied housing; I marched for the African-American, Soviet sympathizer Paul Robeson.

My first roommate moved down a floor to the "socialist wing" of Green hall; my next one moved up a floor to the "lesbian wing." I dated older and smarter guys, like Carl Sagan. And gay guys, who weren't ready to come out. The College held a mock Miss America Beauty Pageant. I was crowned Miss University of Chicago. My talent was a droll recitation of Andrew Marvell's poem, "To his Coy Mistress." I tried peyote. I acted in Compass Players, the precursor to Second City. I became a Platonist before I became an Existentialist. I argued with the Aristotelians. I slept until noon. Occasionally, I went to class.

When my freshmen grades came in, father scolded me. I responded by cutting all my financial dependence on him. I had tuition scholarships, baby-sitting jobs, and a life guard position at Bruno Bettelheim's Orthogenic school for emotionally disturbed children where I earned my pay saving every day at least one child from drowning. I was sixteen.

* * *

Sociology called. I earned a Ph.D. and became a university professor. I married, had two sons, divorced. *That* American story. I moved from Chicago to Colorado to California to where I now live in what some call "fly-over country" but others promote as "the heart of it all"—Ohio.

In 1980, I married Ernest Lockridge—a good match and second marriages for both of us, a *good* American story. Our blended families moved to historical Weybridge, a village founded by New Englanders in 1803. I began a writing-project that has culminated in this book.

The chapters in *Seven Minutes from Home: An American Daughter's Story* tell of my everyday life within seven minutes of my home and they tell of changes in my personal life and the social, cultural and built environments surrounding me. The chapters are arranged in chronological order from 1980 to the present. Although each chapter is narratively complete in itself, the chapters link together to form a larger narrative, a story of an American daughter. Me.

I have followed the ethical writing principles of sociology and have changed people's names and identifying features, including most place names. But I have not changed the names of my immediate family.

I think of the chapters as palimpsests—pictures that, although taken in particular times and places, allow traces of the past to poke through and be visible. The chapters reflect the ways in which people make sense of their worlds, finding traces of the already experienced in their new experiences. As such, how could *Seven Minutes from Home* not *also* be a book about my father—my mother, my family, my friends—as my mind settles upon this *location,* that *location,* then yet another *location?* How can being Chicago born to an oddly configured family not affect how I live my adult life? How can teen years spent in the "libertarian" University of Chicago not affect me? But even as I might mentally travel in time and space, I can always trust myself to return to the *here and now.* The reader can, too.

* * *

Although my body only goes seven minutes from my Weybridge home and my mind scopes out my past and considers my future, my experiences are continuously shaped by the social and cultural world in which I (by dint of being alive) am traveling. I write about those, too. Traveling only seven minutes from home, I live locally in a global world.

People become who they are by what they do in their everyday lives. Although I travel and give writing workshops internationally, in my *everyday* life I spend time with friends, family and neighbors; I go to stores and cultural events; I write and make art. For much of my life, I taught Sociology at The Ohio State University. When I retired, I chronicled some of those experiences in the book, *Fields of Play: Constructing an Academic Life.* This book is not about *that.* It is about constructing a life *outside* the academy seven minutes from home *pre* and *post* retirement. "I am an American woman, Chicago born," and in this book I tell *my* story as an American daughter.

If everyone meditated or wrote about how they live their lives seven minutes from their homes, everyone would be connected in time and space. Now, wouldn't that be brilliant!

NEIGHBORHOODS
1980–2000

Don't choose a house; choose a neighborhood.

– Russian Proverb

SUCH A YELLOW HOUSE

"Shoot him or move." The Columbus police officer is in our living room. "Those are your only options." It is the next day after our teenage neighbor, Lenny, high on PCP and seeing that Ernest's car was not in the driveway, sledge hammered down our front door and tried to rape me.

My yelling got someone to call the Columbus police but because the caller could not identify exactly what house the yelling was coming from the dispatcher declined sending a patrol car.

My yelling woke up on my sons. Twelve-year old Josh, frightened, climbed out his second-floor window. Sixteen-year old Ben saw me on the floor of his bedroom kicking at Lenny. Ben rose up from his bed and came at Lenny with wildness in eyes, arms, fists that I had never seen. Lenny fled.

"Shooting Lenny is the preferred option," the police officer said. He was sick and tired of arresting Lenny and disgusted with the juvenile court system that kept releasing him. "Law," the officer said, "but no order."

We had to move. I needed to live somewhere safe, and where I felt safe. I chose Historical Weybridge. It resembled a Nineteenth Century Currier and Ives etching with its tidy houses, tree-lined streets, and quaint downtown. In my mind, the Nineteenth Century's small town New England was a place where the domestic world was safe.

Only five houses were for sale in Weybridge. I had already rejected four.

"It looks too small," I say about the Cape Cod on Revere Street. Ernest had brought three daughters to our marriage. I had brought two sons and two cats.

"It's bigger than it looks," our realtor says.

"It is so yellow," I protest.

"It can be painted," she counters.

"I like the white picket fence," I say, buying into an American Dream.

"It's an exact replica of one in Williamsburg," she says. "The gate is held shut by a cannonball on a chain."

"The location is good," I say. I ignore the cannonball.

"Want to go inside?"

The inside walls are yellow. Wall-to-wall avocado-green shag carpet cover the floors. But there are five bedrooms, two bathrooms, a sun-room and a finished basement. In the large back yard there is perhaps the last standing American elm. A wood plank swing hangs on ropes from a lower limb. I can't resist. I sit on it, push my feet under me and lean forward and backward, legs out and back.

Swinging back and forth, I remember being seven and swinging so high that I feared I would go over the bar and be turned inside out as my older brother Barrie told me would happen. Swinging back and forth, I remember when I was eight and purposefully hurt my brother for the first and only time. I was pushing him on a swing but when he was up as high as I could reach, I held onto the seat. He tumbled to the ground. I let go of the seat and watched it strike his back and heard him cry-out. He didn't rat on me to our mother. He still has the scar. We both have the memory.

"Laurel?" the realtor calls my name.

"Oh, my sons loved to swing," I say. To myself I chant Robert Louis Stevenson's poem:

> *How do you like to go up in a swing,*
> *Up in the air so blue?*
> *Oh, I do think it the pleasantest thing*
> *Ever a child can do!*

I make an offer. It is accepted.

"Are the neighbors friendly?" I ask our neighbor to the east as we move in.

"After you have lived here for a couple of decades, they might talk to you," he says. He surveys his oddly shaped trees, limbs trimmed off mid-limb.

"But, if my house were on fire, the neighbors would help, wouldn't they? Call the fire department."

"Don't count on it."

COME WALK WITH ME

As Geography without History seemeth a carkasse
without motion; so History without Geography,
wandreth as a Vagrant without a certain habitation.

– Captain John Smith, 1624

Come walk with me out my kitchen door onto the crumbling cement stairs and macadam driveway, past the redbud, petite lavender bush and Japanese maple that replaced the towering silver maple we cut down before it fell down on our now Williamsburg blue-painted and red-roofed Cape Cod home. The Japanese maple's leaves are crimson, its trunk less wide than Black Cat's waist.

When I peek around my garage, I see my backyard neighbor peeking at me through her binoculars. Unwell, she sits in her chair and rarely goes out.

Our standoffish neighbor to the east moved after his wife died of breast cancer. During the last few months of her life a UPS truck daily brought clothes she had ordered from catalogues, clothes she would never wear. "Wasn't she just nuts?" her husband said, in one of his rare loquacious moments. "What was she thinking?" *She wasn't thinking. She was feeling, wanting hope.* "Will you stay in our house during the funeral?" he asked. "You know, to keep things safe. You don't know what burglars might have read the obituary." I agree to stay there. *What was I thinking?*

An eight-foot high wooden fence now separates his property from mine put in immediately upon closing by a single woman, a banker, who moved here from the east coast. She cannot believe what a good house she can get for so little money. Once she starts talking she can't stop. So let's pretend she is not there right now in her short shorts mowing the lawn and stopping traffic. I have nick-named her Show-Butt.

Stand by our white picket fence and wave at Mr. Johnson, a widower walking Fido II around his side-yard. Right now he is multi-tasking, holding the leash while Fido II does his business, and picking up the gum wrappers kids discard on the way to their Weybridge schools. Farms have ceded to the athletic niceties of a suburban school: lacrosse field, indoor and outdoor pools, football stadium, running tracks, soccer field, bike path, and boat house.

Both of my sons went to Weybridge High School. One graduated early, one dropped out.

Come walk further west with me on my street, Revere Street. Bob and Martha moved in two years ago and added a "wing" larger than the original house. The wing obscured our view of the sunset, gave them a view of our bedroom and us a view of their new master suite. We installed shades. They had a baby, Robert. Martha is tending to her flower garden, her head down, and Bob is up a ladder, contemplating something. No need to interrupt.

The small tan 1815 farm house across the street, sitting on a half-acre, is owned by the previous owner of our house, Mr. B. He miswired our house so outlandishly that if Ernest had not been wearing rubber soled shoes and standing on a rubber mat, he would have been fried when he touched the fuse box with a screwdriver. Mr. B. is a safety engineer.

We hope the renter of Mr. B's house is safe. We think perhaps just maybe she is the mistress of one of our state senators, as the senator comes and goes at odd hours in a limo with darkened windows and a single digit license plate. This is the kind of detail my criminal-lawyer father would have noticed. And the kind of intrigue Ernest enjoys imagining.

The "Woman-Who-Steals-Cats" lives in the next house. Black Cat had run out the kitchen door when a meter-reader left it open. We peppered the neighborhood with "Missing Cat" flyers. We called up and down the street, day and night, "Black Cat…Treat… Kitty…Kitty." Three bereft days later, a white-haired woman peeked out her front door at us and bade us come over. "Such a nice cat and so happy to be petted by *me*," she began in a crackly voice. "Of course, I knew that whoever owned her was terrible to her or else why would she be so happy to be petted by *me*? Why would she be such a nice cat?" She pauses, eyes us and continues. "I've seen all your signs up. I guess you care for her. So I've decided to let you have her."

Continue walking west. Admire the tidy green lawns, homey gardens, and frame houses of the residents of Selden Village, the name chosen to honor an early settler. One of his descendents developed the acreage in 1940 with individually designed homes on large lots. Mine is one of them.

Our homes had restrictive covenants to be enforced until January 1, 2000— "no businesses…no noxious activities…no structures less than $5000" and "transfer of deed only to Members of the White Race." Wave to the Japanese couple living in the blue house. Bring a gift for the newly adopted Chinese girl living in the corner house.

Continue walking west until you come to where Revere Street T-bones Lexington Boulevard. There you will see a log cabin on the river's edge, built as a saw mill and a tannery for the logs and hides coming down the River for city-folks in Columbus. In the 1930's a professor bought it, prepared it for year-round living, and invited James Thurber to bunk in. Built over and under and all around ever since, the house is for sale at a reduced price—a mite under six-hundred thou.

Turn left up Lexington Boulevard and smile at the California Ranch MacMansion with its four-car garage, and fifteen car paved side-lot, gazebo, pool, high-rise pool house, life-sized Buddha, and say, "Hi, Guys," to whichever crew of workmen happen to be working on the grounds.

Look all the way up Lexington Boulevard and imagine you are in the middle of a five square mile tract of once wooded acres teeming with wildlife and wild berries, land traversed by pre-historic and wild horses, and contested over by a montage of Native American tribes: Ancient Ones, Adena, Hopewell, Late Woodland, Chippewa, Delaware, Eel River, Iroquois, Kaskaskia, Miami, Mingo, Munsee, Ottawa, Piankashaw, Potawatomi, Sauk, Seneca, Shawnee, Wea, and Wyandot. My son Ben found an arrowhead in our back yard. No Native American tribes living here now.

Concerned about the "Indian Wars," Congress passed an act giving land to two groups, those who had given "Military Service" and to the "United Brethren who had propagated the Gospel among the Heathen." Further congressional acts divided the land into tracts of 4,000 acres. In 1790, President John Adams deeded 4,000 acres to Reverend John Dunlop. My house is in this tract.

My house's history is recorded in the title I rescued five years-ago from the garbage bin atop others of its kind. My title! "After verification, we always throw those old papers away," the Chicago title and Trust loan officer told me.

I count myself lucky to have more than verification: 137 pages of American history that I've read from beginning to end. The 4,000 acre tract was sold for $5000 to a Connecticut consortium. They planned a New England village—schools, farms, library, Episcopal church, Masonic Lodge, common holdings, private holdings—and a New England way of life. All this Americana before any of them had set foot in Native American land, Ohio.

Let's continue our walk on Lexington Boulevard. Here sweeping half-acre front lawns surround grand houses, built fifty-years ago. Both sides of the street are lined with oak trees, planted at equal intervals. "Well, isn't this

15

something," Ernest's mother would declare in her Hoosier accent when she visited and we would walk her down this "stretch."

On your left is the "circle," a miniature green valley surrounded by oaks that conceal the goings-on there, like my teen-aged son and his teen-aged girl-friend, sometimes star-gazing. Mostly not.

Don't look to your right at the "black-faced lawn jockey" in front of that manor house. Weybridge was part of the Underground Railroad and history confirms that "Jockos" marked safe houses, but I doubt the owner has a clue. Instead, look to your left, at the faux brick ranch where my Women's Liberation Group met until her husband forbade it.

Seven minutes from my home, and you've come upon the Secret Wilderness. You walk over fallen limbs, under bent-over trees, under a canopy of leaves and over a path of fallen-ones. If you walk for a quarter hour in and out of bramble you reach the River, where branches flow with crickety music over stones that memorialize millennia of stories.

ERRANDS BY FOOT

Seventy degrees, sunny, dry and leafy. A perfect afternoon for doing errands on foot. Living almost in Old Weybridge I can walk to downtown places on High Street in less than seven minutes. Today, while Ernest mows the lawn and the cats nap on the sun porch, I will spend several hours, alone, going and doing. My list:

1. HNB National Bank
   Friday is "Customer Appreciation Day."
   Will I get a free sample?

2. Weybridge Library
   Browse the new novels at the brand-new library, a modern glass and brick affair.

3. Dairy Queen
   Peanut Buster Parfait.

4. Village Green
   Sit, spoon, sketch.

5. Christian Science Reading Room
   There they are, the pages of the day, lit up, just like the pages were in the Christian Science Reading Room window near our home in Chicago. Father's Christian Scientist Aunt taught him to forego medicines. He taught me that, too. I had my first aspirin the evening after teaching my first class.

6. Care Uniforms window
   This little store's window is dizzy-making with its pastel colored scrubs, some with teddy bears or kittens printed willy-nilly all over the tops. The white uniforms once worn by nurses so they'd look nun like, demure or angelic, have been replaced by scrubs. Orderlies, technicians, aides, maintenance, housekeeping and

dietary staff all wear scrubs. Everyone looks alike in the medical world except for the doctors, who wear white lab coats and shirts with silk ties.

7. Allan's Drug Store

"Let's see, Laurel," Pharmacist Allen checks his index-cards. "You're ready for a refill." "And a Hershey bar, too," I say. "We're a pharmacy," Mr. Allen laughs. "You know we don't carry candy."

8. Weybridge Hardware

Such a cavernous store. It takes up much of the block in the middle of downtown Weybridge. It dates to the late 1800s. It is like an old-fashioned general store. One section is devoted to pots and pans and crockpots and dishes; another to garden gnomes, seeds and stakes; a third to all things a house might need to become a home, including pet supplies; and a fourth huge section has aisles upon aisles of stacks of drawers, each drawer holding different screws or tacks or thingamajigs. Old men in suspenders chat me up. "So, how's your lawn doing on that fertilizer your Mister bought? Do you need some more keys? Light bulbs? Cat kibble?" I can get anything here. Even a Hershey bar.

9. Curio Cabinet

This is the place to find a birthday present for my sister, Jessica. She collects all things porcelain or crystal. I choose a little crystal horse and Miss Betty gift wraps it for me. I browse the Dickens Christmas Village, all year set-up with twinkling lights, a miniature of what downtown Weybridge looks like come December. White lights are strung along High Street from its gas-light-looking fixtures. Store owners' deck out their windows in greenery, fake snow and mysteriously wrapped boxes. In the Village Green, a forty-foot Christmas Tree towers over a fenced-in space with statues of Joseph, Mary and Baby Jesus asleep in a manger. A live donkey with a blanket on its back. Live lambs greeting children with "baa-baa's."

10. The Weybridge Inn

The building is lovely to look upon with its fine front porch, side garden and mansard roof. Since 1842 it has been a "traveler's inn," at first offering dinners for a dime, lodging for a quarter. Now the

Inn has fallen on hard times. No rooms are rentable and the steam-heated buffet food, which my sons and I had one Thanksgiving after my divorce from Herb, is odious.

11. Moody's Paper Supply
     Get mailing box for the crystal horse.

12. Post-Office
     Mail crystal horse.

13. The Doll House
     Drool over the antique dolls. Lust.

14. Home Market
     "Hi, Jeb," I say to the butcher. "We'll take a couple pounds of beef-stew and—that chicken looks good." "Fresh from our farm," Jeb says. "Oh, and do you have any of your sweet sausage?" "Yep. How many would you like?" "Five, please." And while he wraps up my meat, I pick up fresh vegetables, freshly baked bread, locally-raised catnip and a pie. Beulah rings me up. She adds today's cost to my running tab to be paid at the end of each month.

When I get home, dawdling a bit, the groceries have been delivered, the freshly mown grass smells sweet and the cats greet me, meowing for catnip.

THE BLOCK PARTY

"We might be taking our lives in our hands," Ernest says.

It is five o'clock, and we're going to the Concord Street "Hi-Neighbor Pot-Luck and Block Party," around the corner from our Revere Street home. Earlier this year the people around the corner tried to get our street permanently blockaded to prevent cut-through traffic on theirs. We fought them and won.

This potluck is a sort of a suburban potlatch to heal battle-scars and re-establish neighborhood harmony.

"Do you think they'll call ambulances for us?" Ernest asks.

"They'll have stretchers, I'm sure."

"Maybe we should call in the Cavalry before it's too late."

When my father was seventeen, he lied about his age and joined the U.S. Cavalry under General John J. Pershing. His regiment was pursuing the Mexican Revolution General, Pancho Villa. Villa seized rich folks' land and distributed it to peasants and soldiers; he robbed trains; he printed money; he murdered, raped and plundered; and he crossed the border to attack Columbus, New Mexico. "We never caught him," Father said. "His own people murdered him for reasons of their own. The U.S. Cavalry never caught him," Father would repeat, wistfully, "But I learned to ride, shoot, sew and cook." I think this was the happiest time in my father's life.

"I don't think the Cavalry would help us any," I say to Ernest.

"Too late," Ernest says. "Looks like our Concord Street neighbors got their blockade."

"It's just for today's potluck, Ernest," I say. "Honestly."

We walk past the yellow sawhorses that have closed off both ends of Concord Street. Balloons, tied to the sawhorses, are waving us onward. Ernest is carrying our contribution of stuffed grape-leaves, fresh from Kroger's. Samir, our Lebanese son-in-law, made the real thing. He and Ernest's daughter, Kelly, live in the *real* thing. They sleep behind an electrified barbed-wire fence with a gun beneath the pillow in Mali, West Africa, where he has business interests. In Lebanon, he monitors his parents' house and bomb shelter in a Christian sector north of Beirut. We worry when Kelly visits. Syrian police check-points start at the airport.

21

Going to their wedding in Beirut was the most frightening thing I have ever done. My shoulders were up to my ears in panic. Massage didn't help. I don't like flying, and there was so much of it. I got so tired, my body exhausted by time-zone changes—eight of them, each way—foreign waters, foreign foods. And the possibility of war, of course. That, too. The State Department had already raised the travel-advisory level: "Don't go. The U.S. Embassy cannot protect you."

Most stressful though was knowing I could be immediately arrested in Beirut should the authorities discover I had been to Israel. I had a new passport without the Israel stamp but for all I knew Lebanon kept computer records of tourists to Israel. Maybe their computer knew I am Jewish, a Jewish child who gave to *keren ami* to plant trees in Israel in her name, a Jewish adult whose support of Israeli independence is recorded in Tel Aviv.

I reminded myself that my last name is that of my Gentile father, "Richardson," and that I resemble him. If the Lebanese authorities asked me, I'd have to deny my heritage. I'd have to lie. I shuddered thinking about denial and deceit. It was as if I was mind experimenting with no longer being "half-Jewish," but "entirely Jewish," at risk for insufferable experiences like those experienced by my Russian Jewish mother.

I went to Beirut because Ernest needs were greater than my fears and because, if all went as planned, Samir would have paid the Syrian police sufficient sums to permit us through their check-points unchecked.

"No police check-points—yet," Ernest says, bringing me back to the Concord Street block party.

Yesterday it stormed for twelve hours. Today is a perfect late September day. The sun is shining, humidity is low, birds are twittering, and the grass smells sweet. Dogs, tethered to fence posts, sniff each other. The street is aswarm with pre-school girls on pink scooters, pre-school boys on blue scooters, fathers and school-aged sons playing bean-bag horseshoes, and fathers and school-aged daughters playing mini-disc golf. Women are lounging on lounge chairs. Teenagers are lounging on the grass. Boys are having a how-many-hot-dogs-can-you-eat challenge. Our ten-year old neighbor boy, Robert, is on his seventh, I hear as I pass by.

"What a lot of kids live on this street," I say to Ernest. "No wonder their parents have been concerned with the cut-through traffic."

Ernest grimaces. "Don't they realize that if one of their children needed an ambulance, it couldn't get through?"

My sons grew up in Clintonville in Columbus on a street with eighty-six other kids. We counted them up once. They'd play kick-the-can, hide-and-seek, cops and robbers, spacemen and space monsters on our red brick street. Young girls tended their baby dolls in strollers. Older girls toted Barbies and Kens. Boys rode their mountain bikes to North Park, built forts, and made tree houses in the oaks.

How safe it all seemed. I never worried about my sons—not knowing, then, that a neighborhood flasher routinely flashed the kids. Or that a man convinced six-year old Josh to come into a car but ten-year old Ben bodily prevented it. Or that Ben and Josh strung rope across the street causing cars to buckle into a brake. Or that they blew up wood piles with the explosives they surreptitiously made in the basement. Or that they shorted electric lines to the meanest man on the street, who just happened to be the colleague of mine who had earlier, as chair of the hiring committee, refused to interview me because I had sons, and mothers belonged at home because otherwise their sons would, you know, end up, you know, like his son had, you know, unmarried living with another man in Greenwich Village. Or that Little Mikey set the fire to his garage. Or that Susie liked all the little "doctors" who treated her in her playhouse. Or that Kenneth had "shop-lifting" lists tucked into his boots. Or that Mrs. T. told them all about how happy she was now that she was "sleeping with Jesus." Or that twelve-year olds bought marijuana and beer from the care-taker at the Park of Roses.

"We don't see kids outside on their own anymore, do we?" I comment to Ernest.

"The world's changed," he says.

"Or parents are smarter," I say. My own lack of smarts about the world my sons inhabited shames and embarrasses me. I'm a sociologist. I should have known. But, I am optimistic, permissive, and law-abiding. And, I was then a single mother who was clueless as to what "boys-being-boys" could mean. *Excuses, excuses, excuses.*

More excuses. I grew up on the streets of north side Chicago, near Wrigley Field. Kids owned the streets. The girls played hopscotch and jacks on the street. The boys played stick-ball, marbles, and numbelypeg—a knife throwing game—at school. Boys fought each other and me. Because I was such a snappish little girl, Father made me measure myself against any boy before I got into a fist-fight with him. If I were taller or the same size, I wasn't allowed to fight. "No fair," I would say. "Too bad," Father would say. "Be the underdog and win, if you can." The last fist-fight I had was with a boy probably a half-a-head taller than I and probably two years older. He knocked me down the stairs into the street where he hit me with his fists until I cried "uncle."

23

Both boys and girls roller-skated, skate keys around our necks. All of us rode scooters. Father had made me one of an orange crate attached by wooden strips to skate-wheels. It had a special compartment to hold my books and dolls. We'd have drag races down the slopingest street. In the winter, we rode our sleds down our iced-over cement-steps right into the street. We played tag, statues, red rover, tug of war—and we didn't steal, burn buildings, do drugs—not even cigarettes, until we were older. And the local "flasher" was not a hidden something, but someone our parents assured us was harmless. Mother said, "Just don't look at him."

"No one looks like a flasher at this block party," I comment to Ernest.

"Disappointed?" he asks.

Ernest adds our grape leaves to the tables laden with side dishes—broccoli, broccoli with raisins, broccoli and cauliflower, carrots with dips, potato boats, potato chips, potato poppits, Fritos and a multitude of deserts.

"Hi, Neighbors," says Brent, who is wearing a name-tag and carrying a spear. "Can I fix you a hot dog?" He gestures to his spear.

"Thanks, Neighbor," says Ernest, introducing us while I make our name-tags. We pile food on our paper plates.

"Be sure and get some of the basbousa cake," Brent says. "It's home-made by our newest neighbors." He gestures to an interracial family of four sitting on chairs behind him.

"Hi, Neighbors," I say. The Anglo husband looks to be in his sixties, his beautiful Somalian wife in her mid-thirties. Their two bronze-colored children nod at me. I wonder if the children identify themselves as "black" or "white" or "bi" or African-American. I wonder if they feel pressured to choose an identity that will exclude the heritage of one of their parents. How it is for them?

When I was growing up—half Jewish/half Gentile—communities labeled me not half and half, but one or the other. At Anshe Emet Synagogue, where I went to Sunday School, I was considered Gentile and excluded from the social-events lest one of the boys become interested in me. At Protestant Family Camp where we spent our summers, I was marginalized and publicly embarrassed by my refusal to say that "Jesus loves me." At the start of each school year, I would count how many children in my class were Jewish and how many were Gentile. Finding the numbers equal confirmed my megalomaniac belief that I had been chosen to bring peace between the tribes.

Brent slides a piece of basbousa on my plate. "Our new neighbor escaped the perpetual Somalian tribal wars."

24

"Talk about block parties," Ernest says. "In Mogadishu it's warfare block-by-block."

"Hello, Neighbors," I say to our Revere Street next-door neighbors, Bob and Martha. We've watched their son Robert grow up and out and up. Martha gestures for us to join them on the grass.

"Which hot dog are you on, Robert?" I ask.

"Just my eleventh," he says. "The competition is pretty stiff."

Ernest holds my plate while I unfold myself, dropping into the grass, tumbling backwards into a bumbling partial back-somersault. I was never a poster-child for flexibility, but I did not so very long ago get down and up somewhat gracefully. Aging, as Ernest reminds me, is better than the alternative. He doesn't have any trouble joining me on the grass, but then he's closer to the ground than I am and he's two-years younger. *Excuses, excuses.*

"Has Robert chosen his Halloween costume yet?" I ask Martha. I've seen him costumed as a Roman soldier, a Viking warrior, a Renaissance knight and Superman.

"He's fluctuating between *Barney Flintstone* and *The Terminator,*" Bob says.

"The history of the world from rock to rockets," Ernest says. "Maybe when he's grown up, he'll join the C.I.A. Our very own home-grown spy!"

"One of my friends is in the C.I.A.," I volunteer. "So is her husband, but in a different division. They have two kids. Now, she's been deployed to Iraq—just her—for three years."

"My nephew's an E.M.T. in Iraq," Brent says. "He's paid in six-figures."

"Army pay?" Ernest says. "Wow!"

"Combat has its rewards," Brent says.

"Yeah!" Ernest says. "We just saw *Universal Soldier.* Vietnam soldiers die but they are brought back to life as near-perfect soldiers. Talk about rewards! Life Ever After!"

"No! No! No," screams a pink helmeted little girl as a police car slips between the saw horses and pulls into the block party.

"She's afraid her little brother is being arrested," her father explains as he scoops her up and carries her to the cruiser.

"It's complicated," Bob tells us, shaking his head. "Her older brother had a freak accident on a ski slope that had been closed for the season. When the police took him to the hospital, she thought he was being arrested. He died that night."

"It's okay," I hear the father say to his pink-helmeted daughter. "Let's go see."

The police-officer turns on his blue and white flashing lights. He gets out and opens all four doors. Kids crawl in and out of the cruiser. He gives each one a little badge. A small boy, a tiny Mercury, races past us with his hands over his ears and tells us to cover ours. Too late. The cruiser's siren blasts. *Ouch!* A white Scottie dog breaks off its leash, whines and tries to kiss me. His owner calls for him, "MacDuff! Come, MacDuff!"

"Enough," Ernest says, calming the dog, talking to him. "MacDuff, do you know that 'enough' was Macbeth's last word?"

Brent begins reciting, "I will not yield to kiss the ground before young Malcolm's feet."

Our neighbor Bob joins in. "And to be baited with rabble's curse."

"Though Birnam Wood be come to Dunsinane," Ernest adds.

"And thou opposed being of no woman born," say all three men in unison. "Yet I will try the last. Before my body I throw my warlike shield." Bob holds his empty paper plate to his chest. Robert makes faces. Brent waves his fork. Ernest rises from the grass, "Lay on, MacDuff. And damned be him that first cries, 'Hold. Enough.'"

The three men look jubilant. Listening to them—taking turns, speaking in harmony—I think this is really a good way for men to bond. Why don't they do it this way more often?

"Were you an English major, too? Like Bob and Ernest?" I ask Brent. I am always surprised when people—other than Ernest—can recite chapter and verse of whatever, whenever.

"No, but I came from a bookish family," Brent says. "The first time they met my wife-to-be they asked her to name Jane Austen's six novels."

"Seven," Bob says.

"The seventh was incomplete," Ernest adds. "I guess I came from a bookish family, too."

I nod. His grandfather did site-recitals at historic sites and wrote history books for children. I read *La Salle* in fourth grade. Ernest's father wrote the best-seller, *Raintree County*, before he committed suicide. Ernest is a novelist, too, and professor of creative writing and English literature. His "office" at home has half-dozen bookcases, floor-to-ceiling, wall-to-wall, crammed with books some of which he culled from his family's collections.

Sometimes I feel envious, sometimes looking at his books makes me aware of what I did not have growing up. Our family did not have book cases or even book shelves. Mother used the lending library and us kids the public one. If it weren't for gifts from my Aunt Laura, I would not have owned any books. My parents never read to me. *Mother Goose?* No. Grimm's fairy tales? Thankfully, no. Father, who was as smart a man as I have ever met, devoured Perry Mason mysteries, maybe getting tips for his work, before I was born, as a criminal-attorney in Al Capone's stable.

Pre-schoolers begin riding their scooters to their homes. Older children are high-fiving. Brent is collecting paper plates. Women are taking their food offerings from the potlatch tables. Ernest helps me up. It is dusk. It is 7:30.

"Life's but a walking shadow, a poor player that struts and frets his hour upon the stage," recites Bob as we walk towards Revere Street.

Ernest joins in, "And then is heard no more."

BLUE WEDNESDAY

The Church's lot is full and most of the streets in this university district are now requiring parking permits. I have driven seven minutes south and slightly east of my Weybridge home back into the university neighborhood I had lived in twenty-five years ago when I first came to Columbus with my then husband Herb, my three-year old son, Ben, not-yet born Josh and Kitty-Cat. We rented half a 1920's brick duplex on Lane Avenue. Neighbors shared hand-push lawn-mowers, baby-sitting and a swing-set in our backyard. Kitty-Cat had alley cat friends. We could walk to the park, the drugstore and The Ohio State University where Herb was a professor of mathematics and I was a post-doc in medical sociology. Now, I can't find a parking space.

When Josh was six-months old, an eviction notice landed in our mailbox. Our landlord sheepishly admitted that he had been negotiating the sale of the property when he had rented to us, and that was why he didn't offer us a lease. We had two weeks to move. A cherry-picker chopped-down the century old oak trees and the vintage swing-set in our back yard. A bull-dozer arrived, remained positioned towards Ben's bedroom. He had nightmares. We moved. The brick duplex was razed. Twelve concrete-block student apartments were built on that treeless corner lot.

Now, all the free-standing homes and duplexes on my old street are gone. Now, the narrow brick roads are one-way streets. Beer bottles, Domino Pizza boxes, and plastic snack-food wrappers surround massive green garbage receptacles, graffiti laden. Three-hundred gallon monsters—large enough to hold a week or two of trash if only the students would use them. Piles of unclaimed *Lanterns* (the students' newspaper) decompose on one street corner. Tattered notices flutter from phone poles. Blue emergency lights blink. Rusting pick-up trucks and old Fords parked bumper to bumper line the curbs. In the alleys they are parked three deep. A torn American flag flies out a window. A young driver in a red baseball cap in a red car rides my bumper, honks, and yells something nasty into his windshield, judging from his one-finger salute. The horizon is lost in the gray of the sky, the gray of the concrete.

I'm about to give up hope when a beat-up red truck pulls out of an unrestricted parking spot a few yards from the Church. It is 3:56 on a chilly Wednesday afternoon. The funeral starts at 4:00.

I sign the Remembrance Book that rests on a small lectern, walk past two bulletin boards with family pictures, and settle into a dark olivewood pew. The blue of heaven surrounds me.

Blue, blue, blue. Blue is the color of the stained glass windows rising nearly to the cathedral ceiling on three walls of the sanctuary. When I was a little girl I thought only blue-eyed children could wear blue. I loved blue. Sky blue. Peacock blue. Powder blue. Navy blue. Prussian blue was my favorite crayon. Wonderful blue eyes. Alas, mine are brown.

Love at first sight: my beloved Blue Point Siamese cat, elegantly perched at the pinnacle of a large cat cage in Weybridge's *PetCenter*, ignoring the posse of fuzzy kittens worshipping at his paws. I took him in my arms and he purred. "How much does this kitten cost?" I asked the high-schooler minding the store. "Siamese cats are $200.00," she said without looking up. I winced, phoned Ernest who came to the mall, and declared, "We have to rescue that cat. He's royalty." Within the hour we had brought a purring Blue Prince to our home in Weybridge.

"Oh no!" Dr. Tompkins, our vet, said when we brought Blue the next day for a check-up. "No. No. No."

"Is he sick?" I asked, tearing up.

"On the contrary," Dr. Tompkins said. "I own that pet store and he was just there for a few hours. He was not for sale. His pedigree is longer than my arm. Both his sire and dam are National Winners. He could sire a dynasty of champions."

"I guess that's not going to happen," I said, holding the purr-box close to myheart.

Dr. Tompkins stared at Blue Prince. "Oh, his look is too sweet, now. He's changed. He won't have the right temperament to sire champions. So let's set a date for his chipping and neutering."

Once Blue was chipped and neutered, we decided to let him be an indoor and outdoor cat. His territory was our yard and the bushes on the other side of our backyard fence, where the elderly man and his house-bound wife lived. When we first moved into our house—before Blue joined us—a noxious smell emanated from their backyard. The elderly man was tapping a foul-smelling water well and had been doing so for decades, despite its illegality. He refused to close the well and we brought the police into the matter. Worse, from his point of view, we had planted a row of leather leaf viburnum along our shared fence, obscuring his ailing wife's window on the world: *our* comings and goings, eatings and drinkings.

On his moving day, after his wife's death, the old man made good on his oft-spoken threat. He poisoned Blue. We found him, stiff and white by the fence. At first I was in denial. "That can't be Blue. It must be some other cat." Then, I was hysterical, crazed with a grief greater than the ones I had expressed at my parents' deaths. Blue was so innocent, young, and beautiful. My companion.

We buried Blue in the backyard under his favorite bird feeder and marked his grave with a plasti-stone, "Creatures great and small." My grief has abated but has not disappeared. When we got the domestic gray cat, Maxwell, from the humane society, only Ernest signed the adoption papers. I just couldn't let another cat into my life. In time, Maxwell has joined Blue Prince under the bird feeder. So has Black Cat. And Capuchin.

I am ashamed of myself for thinking about the lives and deaths of my cats. But maybe that is what other people do at funerals of the people they aren't as close to as they are to their—dare I say it?—pets.

* * *

This is my first Christian funeral. Reverend Russell has already begun the service. He looks like a nonagenarian, small, skinny, bald pate barely showing above the lectern. Behind him is an alter, small floral displays, a cross made from woven straw, and an organ with a red-robed organist, facing away from the congregation. There is no casket.

The Reverend speaks in a crackly, yet soothing voice, in oratorical rhythms—phrase, pause, phrase, pause. Looking at the widow, he says, "Whether alive or dead, we belong to Jesus." Long pause. "There is eternal life for Matthew Blair," the Reverend sighs deeply and looks at the family. "You will feel his presence for days." *Only for days*? That is not enough time. I still feel Blue Prince's presence, hovering, Can I find him in the windows, like I do in the clouds?

"A band of angels have come," the Reverend says, his head bowed. I look around. I wonder if he sees *angel* angels with wings and halos. *Can animals be angels*?

"Let us sing *The Lord is my Shepherd*—number 143," the Reverend says, bringing me out of my Wandering Jew mind.

"Its number 145!" The organist's baritone booms out.

"Yes—145," Reverend Russell agrees, and then as an afterthought, as if nudged by a buried body-memory, he turns his palms upward and lifts his arms to the ceiling. The congregation rises. He lowers his arms and adjusts his coat sleeves. We sing three hymns, four verses each. After each first verse singing the soprano melody line, I go to the alto part, into my comfort zone, singing the meditative, repetitious pleasure of middle D, my favorite note, and then ending with the predictable, reassuring resolution—E-A-D. I have never heard any of these hymns before, but I am entranced with how easily they can be sung, how gracious their melodic invitation, how comforted I feel.

Reverend Russell pushes his palms toward the floor. The congregation sits. "I've chosen three readings," he says. "A psalm from the Old Testament, a reading from the Book of James and one from the Gospel." Three worn books sit on the lectern. He picks up one, reads a Psalm and hands the book to the widow. She nods. I try to hear the words but my mind follows my gaze into the blue stained-glass window behind him. *Ah! There's Blue Prince! Is this what people do in churches? Find loved ones in the stained glass?*

Stain = Sin? My old neighbor sinning, staining, poisoning Blue. *Hi Blue, you Angel you...*

I had learned in Anshe Emet Sunday School that idolatry was a sin. Is idolatry putting anything made by humans above God? Anything? Everything? Writing, grieving, talking, singing, thinking? So, in this moment am I sinning? Caught in my own thoughts? Disappearing into blueness?

Maybe I am "sinning" just by breaking some cultural trust that at a funeral one *acts as if* one is mournful. Well, I am. Mournful about the killing of helpless animals. Grief-stricken over poisoned Blue. Blue. Blue.

Three generations of the bereaved family sit in the first pews, behind them a row of handsome young men, some bronze, some fair, some dark-skinned, all cleanly shaven. Many pews hold aging men in hand-tailored merino wool suits sitting beside non-trophy wives, sweet-looking women of a certain age in silk designer suits. Throughout the pews clusters of women sit together. I myself am in such a cluster, sitting next to an ex-member— fallen member?—of my Women's Liberation Group to which the widow, Florence, belongs and the reason I am here, not Matthew. I love Florence. We have known each other for decades. She trusts me.

I hold a special place in her heart.

Matthew's daughter comes to the podium representing the family. She reads an email from her son, John, who is in the Peace Corps. I remember the story that Florence wrote about John's birth and her plan to write about each subsequent grandchild. Have they all made turns to the good like John? Or, has she had to suffer the little children, as others in our group have?

A middle-aged man in an expensive-looking suit rises and walks to the lectern. "Matthew Blair served on the Board of Trustees for twenty years," he tells us. "Matt always asked the same questions: 'How are we treating our people? Are they paid well?' He had to miss the last board meeting but phoned us and said, 'Please don't underestimate my spirit.'"

"Matthew knew every rule in the Ohio Code and encouraged everyone in the firm to learn them," one of his business partners testifies.

"He gave financial advice to the caddies for free," a PGA official says. He points to the row of clean-shaven young men of different races, looking alike in their PGA blue sports-coats.

"Major Blair was one of the Greatest Generation," says a weary-looking old man. Some of the congregants nod their assent. Others gasp at his military rank.

"Mr. Blair put God's love into action by bringing people together to build homes, communities and hope," reads a man with a West African accent.

Florence had married a good man, a hero. And, I didn't know beans about him until now. Maybe that is the gift of a funeral—to introduce us to the deceased in ways that inspire and don't let us "underestimate his spirit."

A white-haired Deaconess slowly winds her way to the podium. It pains me to watch her pain. She raises her hand, palms up, and affirms, "Flights of angels sing Matthew Blair to his rest."

On cue, the organist begins playing the Prelude from Bach's The Well-Tempered Clavier, music I know well, music that long-ago I had compulsively used to settle me down, encourage me, inspire me, focus me, because I was writing my dissertation, nursing baby Ben, and denying that my then-husband's homebrew making and drinking would destroy our marriage.

Like flights of angels, caddies rise and escort us, pew-by-pew, giving everyone an opportunity to talk about themselves or give their condolences to the family waiting in a long-line in the vestibule, How hard that must be for the family. And how dark this space is compared to the bright blueness of the sanctuary.

"Florence," I say giving her a hug. I have no other words.

"Thank you for coming, Laurel," Florence says. She looks so sweet and staunch. "Meet my brother, Garth." He's looks like Florence but taller, grayer, and more wrinkled. He is wearing a blue serge jacket, similar to hers, too. "Garth, this is my *dearest* friend, Laurel. I've told you about her."

33

"Hello," he says, averting his eyes. He does not try to shake my hand, for which I am grateful. He turns his shoulder away from me, cups his mouth and whispers something in Florence's ear.

"Yes, *that* friend," she half-whispers back.

She nods at me. I nod back.

The siblings grew up in Kansas on an apple orchard called *Eden's Acres.* Their parents were serious, strict and pious, prototypes of *American Gothic.* During the summers, Garth and Florence spent almost all their time together swimming, feeding ducks, carving fallen apples into grotesques. Garth was Florence's mentor, protector, confidante. When she was twelve and he sixteen, he led her to a grotto on the edge of the orchard and raped her. By the time she was fourteen, wanting his attention and love, she was the one initiating the contacts. Then he left for college. He married. She married. She never told Matthew.

She said I was the only one she ever told.

* * *

Leaving the Church, I walk around the rubble surrounding it toward my car. "Oh, hell!" I swear. My car has been parked in by a motorcycle fit into that little extra space the red truck had occupied before I parked my car. "Ouch," I shout after kicking the front tire of the motorcycle.

"Do you need some help?" A band of blue-jacketed caddies from the funeral have seen my plight.

"Lend me your keys," one says.

"Nah," shouts another, flexing his muscles and pointing to the motorcycle. "Let's do it…let's get this baby out of the way…1-2-3…lift." The young men drop the motorcycle, catawampus partially in the gutter, partially on the sidewalk. It blends in perfectly with the other detritus.

"Thanks, Angels," I say, getting into my getaway car.

SECOND ACTS

If Ernest and I make all the green lights by driving five-miles over the speed limit south down High Street, in less than seven minutes we will reach the Areopagetica Second-Hand Book Store, in Clintonville where I lived fifteen years ago. I moved there after my duplex in the university district was razed.

Named for the tract written by John Milton defending freedom of speech Areopagetica Bookstore is new to Clintonville but has already become the cultural center for the emerging hippified and academized block of stores—Momentum Health Store, Audio Wright Gallery, Wine Makers Supplies and Pearls of Wisdom. These have replaced the old neighborhood's drugstore, pharmacy, Flippo's Fast Food, Sangler Sewing Center, Mr. Fix-It, Bob's Keys, Van's Music Supply and the bowling alley.

My sons, Ben and Josh, walked to all those places when we lived two blocks away on the east bank of the Olentangy River. Our nineteenth-century house had a black slate roof, red-oak floors, and leaded glass windows. Heirloom rose bushes. An antique horseshoe over the garage door was held in place with seven antique nails. I still miss it; I love describing it.

One winter the river froze over and we skated for miles upstream. Each autumn we piled leaves into mounds for the kids to dive into from their Creative Playthings geodesic monkey bars. The boys could walk to school, crossing under High Street through a tunnel, now closed because children could be abducted from it.

Mother died of breast cancer and Father came to visit. He mortared the brick steps as a stop-gap fix and took three-year old Josh on walks. Josh would touch his third finger to his thumb, open and close, open and close. He said he was talking to the butterflies.

Neighbors came for coffee and gossip. I taught my graduate seminars there and my Women's Liberation Group and Women's Poetry Workshop met there. I wrote books, papers, and poems on the glassed-in sleeping porch. Looking in on me one glorious summer morning, the window-washer said he felt sorry for me having to work inside. At night, I'd sit on the floor in the breakfast room, smoking my Benson and Hedges, often purchased for me at Steve's by one of my underage sons. They'd hand over the two-quarters and unfurl my hand-written permission note. Once Josh got back a nickel too much in change. He walked home and then back to return the unearned money. Steve let him keep it. I stayed tethered to the house's one telephone, talking long distance, connecting to my past.

On July 4th of 1970, I received a phone-call from my sister Jessica. Our father was dead. She, my brother-in-law John, my brother Barrie and I met at the Miami airport and drove to Father's condo in Key Biscayne. When we arrived, the door was still sealed shut with a bright yellow "Crime-Scene" tape. We waited until a homicide officer came; he told us we could not enter and that we should make reservations at a hotel for the night. The next day, when we gained entry into the condo, Father's body had been taken to the morgue. I never saw it.

Although Father had been writing his memoirs as a lawyer for Al Capone, an Illinois State Prosecutor, a failed Congressional candidate, campaign manager for Senator Everett Dirksen and ardent believer that President Nixon was a "mafia puppet," there was not a piece of writing paper, written on or blank, in the condo. No Father's Day cards either. But on his writing desk *The Miami Herald* was opened to an article headlined, "One of Villa's Guards Buried: 'Not Many are Left Now.'" One pallbearer, a Villa body guard, said, "We were very young…We were bad soldiers…but we were brave fighters." I wonder if the news article brought Father back to that happiest time in his life when he was in the U.S. Cavalry chasing Pancho Villa. Or, if it felt ominous.

After my father's death, I called a Chicago criminal attorney that my family knew. I told him the story of the homicide tape, missing papers and missing dead body. The lawyer confirmed that Father had been at multiple risks. Key Biscayne was Nixon country, ex-pat Mexican country, and ex-Chicago mob country. He said he'd check on Father's death and get back to me. He did. "Laurel," he said, "you have a house and a husband in Columbus. Let it go."

A month later, I filed for divorce from my children's father, Herb. Father's death freed me to leave an untenable marriage. Father defended every accused criminal, but he opposed divorce. "It was the worse crime of all," he said. His opposition to divorce had never dwindled, and my fear of his disapproval never had either.

Ohio did not have no-fault divorces. I needed witnesses. On Good Friday morning, three friends joined me for the drive to the courthouse. "A divorce must be very heavy," said five-year old Josh. "To need so many people to help carry it."

Then, a lot of even heavier things happened. On the first Halloween night after my divorce, I was an extremely reluctant passenger in a friend's Volkswagen. My intuition told me not to go. But I did. When we were stopped for a red-light, I reached for the door handle. "I'm out of here," I shouted. Too late. So that's why it's called *blacking out*, I thought. Everything was black, no nuances of deep purples or Prussian blues. No slices of lamp light. We had been hit from behind by a drunken driver. My head went through the windshield, then, somehow, my leg. My cheek was broken, my jaw broken, my right eye pulsed on my cheek. Or, so the doctor told me when I came out of my coma. All I remember from the coma is ten-year old Ben hiding by the side of my hospital bed chanting, "Don't go, Mom...I can't take care of Josh...Come back."

A year later my sister Jessica gave me money to redecorate. I hired a painter and fired him. He was more interested in making me, than making my house over. A young roofer, untethered, fell off the roof. He left on a gurney. I had nightmares. During the blizzard of 1978, when the wind never abated as if the storm was breathing out, never in, Ben complained of severe chest pain. I drove him to the hospital where he had an x-ray and was sent home. Early the next morning, a radiologist phoned. Ben had been misdiagnosed. He had a totally collapsed lung. He could die.

Dr. Nail, a hand surgeon, slammed his Mercedes into my two-hundred year old oak tree and blamed the tree for its own demise. He sued me. My insurance agent tried to "comfort" me.

Our newish neighbor boy Lenny stole Josh's bike and left it at a house break-in. Lenny sledge hammered his sister's car, threatened Ben and Ernest's oldest daughter, Susan, with the same. These were preludes to Lenny's attack on me that precipitated our move to the small yellow Cape Cod house in Weybridge where our blended family could be safe.

All this before there was an Areopagetica Second-Hand Book Store.

* * *

"Lots of books here," I say to Ernest.

"Twenty-percent off all books, for the month of July," Ernest says, reading the sandwich board just inside the door.

"I love the smell," I say, sniffing Areopagitica's air. "Books mellowing." No matter where the used-book store, no matter its holdings, the smell is the same. Familiar and comforting. Not like those paperless new-fangled CD's.

37

"Welcome. I'm Kevin." Kevin, a pony-tailed bearded man leads us toward the back of the bookstore. It is hot. "I assume you're here for Liz James's poetry reading."

I am struck by the orderliness and abundance of the stacks. *History, Philosophy, Literature.* Shelves labeled and books neat upon them. *Austen, Dickens, Fitzgerald.* I spy a copy of HOWL in the Rare Book glassed-front cabinet.

"What does it cost?" I ask Kevin, pointing to it.

"A thousand dollars," Kevin says. "It's signed by Ginsberg and Ferenghetti."

"You had one, didn't you?" Ernest asks me.

"I did. A first edition signed by Ginsberg to me at a poetry reading at the Northern Lights Bookstore in San Francisco." I was 19, a University of Chicago college graduate, living on my own two-thousand miles from friends and family. I had so wanted to go to California but once there, my world truncated into one of marijuana, pretense, sports cars, rich boyfriends—and intense feelings of despair and anomie. I was too young for the life I had chosen.

Ten or so years later I gave my copy of HOWL to some visiting poet at Denison University where I was teaching. I don't remember which poet or why. Probably to enhance my status, showing the visitor that I wasn't just another middle-class know-nothing Mid-Westerner teaching sociology at a fair-to-middling university.

"Wow! They've got Fitzgerald's *The Crack-up,*" Ernest says. "Do you know about it?"

"Not really," I equivocate.

"It's posthumous. Edmund Wilson put it together from Fitzgerald's notebooks."

"I hope nobody does that to me."

"It's where Fitzgerald writes, 'There are no second acts in American lives.'"

"Oh," I say. I've heard Ernest quote this line before.

"Here you are." Kevin gestures to the thirty or so chairs arranged around a podium. A library table is set with punch, hot-water, Nescafe and cookies. We sign the Readers Book and take the last two chairs.

"So glad you could come," says Liz, giving each of us a cheek-kiss. Liz and I have been together in the Women's Poetry Workshop for decades. Before then, Liz was a "returning" graduate student. Ernest, a professor of creative writing, awarded one of her poems a major prize. Liz is one of my top-two favorite Columbus poets.

"It's 7:30, Liz," Dianne, the organizer of the poetry series says.

"Glad you could come on this hot July evening," Liz says. She adjusts her Arabian tunic and exotic reading glasses. She is carrying, girl style, a tattered magazine. She is in her late fifties, but keeps her hair blond and perky. Her voice is sweet and soft. "At my last reading," she begins, "I read my recently published poems. This time I want to read my favorite poem—the best poem ever written—at least that is what I think and have thought since I was twelve…And, it has had a major influence on me." She fumbles through her magazine, *Poets and Writers,* and I see she has pasted poems on its pages. *What a clever way to keep and recycle.*

"Here," Liz says, "Keats' *On First Looking into Chapman's Homer.*" She reads:

> Much have I travell'd in the realms of gold,
> And many goodly states and kingdoms seen.
> Round many western islands have I been
> Which bards in fealty to Apollo hold…

Liz keeps reading but I stop listening. I blank out. I remember reading the poem in college, but is hasn't stuck with me. Perhaps, I didn't understand it. Probably, it wasn't taught. Maybe I missed that class. Maybe the professor didn't understand it. I don't understand it now, either.

Perhaps Liz sees my blanked-out face or perhaps it has nothing to do with me when Liz says, "I want to read it again." This time, I pay attention all the way to the end of the poem:

> Or like stout Cortez when with eagle eyes
> He star'd at the Pacific—and all his men
> Look'd at each other with a wild surmise—
> Silent, upon a peak in Darien.

"That pause, after '*silent*'… it always give me chills. *Silent.*" Liz looks exalted.

"Keats died when he was twenty-five," Ernest whispers to me.

When I was twenty-five, I had a marriage, child, Ph.D., and a faculty position at Cal-State- Los Angeles. *What new could ever happen to me?* I thought my life had peaked; was over. Keats's was.

"So young," I say, shaking my head.

"Now, here's the poem I wrote inspired by Keats," Liz announces, coming down from the imagined peak. "You may not see the connection, but there is one." She opens her magazine and selects a poem she had pasted in it, a poem about walking on her street and seeing the trees. I don't see the connection, but I love the poem.

"Okay, now we are going to have a writing exercise," Liz says. Dianne hands out pencils and paper. Liz reads a series of oxymorons and instructs us to write them on our paper: *jumbo shrimp; tight slacks; black light; boneless ribs; civil war; natural make-up; veggie burger; bittersweet.* She tells us, "Circle three that you like, pass your paper to the left, and write something using the oxymora circled by your neighbor."

I am clearly confused about having a definitely unexpected writing exercise at a poetry reading and I am planning to turn a blind eye to the fine mess I have partially completed on the copy paper.

"Now read your pieces aloud," Liz says.

"I stand down," I say. "My creative juices are mighty weak."

"C'mon, Laurel," Ernest says, "I imagine they're somewhat awesome."

"False hope," I say to my Ernest, my larger-half. "What terribly fine writing did you produce?"

"None," he says. "And that's the relative truth."

He folds his paper and puts it in his jeans' pocket. Sight unseen, he thinks, but I'll read it when we get home. Others read their oxymoronic writings.

"Acutely dull," I whisper to Ernest.

"Indecent exposure," he whispers back.

"Same difference."

"Almost done?" Dianne asks the group.

"All instant classics," announces Ernest.

"Yes, they were awfully good," Liz says. She winks at Ernest.

"Open-mike time," Dianne says. "We're running late and there are nine people who want to read. Ernest and I are two of them. A retired professor reads two Auden poems about freedom, because this is July. Emma reads women's freedom poems, because this is July and that's when Elizabeth Cady Stanton at the Seneca Falls Convention in 1840 submitted "that all men and woman are created equal." Betsy reads her free-verse. A red-headed woman reads anti-War poems; her gray-bearded husband reads anti-Peace ones. A wiry young man reads a long, amusing hand-written poem called "HELP!" The poem begins with the "help desk" and builds to a catastrophic conclusion—lack of breathable air, drinkable water, tillable soil. I want to hear it a second time.

"Please everyone read just one poem," Dianne interjects. "One time only."

Ernest's turn. He reads Frost's *Desert Places,* the dark twin, he had told me earlier, of the well-known *Stopping by Woods on a Snowy Evening.* Ernest reads so well. I am almost in tears. He relays the commonsense of the poem and its structure. I can understand this poem: No matter how frightened the narrator might be by the lonely unknown spaces in and between the stars, it is nothing like the scary lonely "desert spaces" inside of him. *Not now,* I am thinking, *not now. I will not go into my lonely scary inside spaces. Not now. I was there in California. Not now. Not now.*

"Laurel?" Dianne calls my name, breaking my reverie.

I stand fast and read my award-winning poem:

IF I WERE A FORK

I would know my place. To the left
of the plate, tines beckoning a hand
to cradle me, me holding meat
for the knife. The blade slips
between my tines, scraping edges.
But there is no pain.

After,

I am bathed in fresh water
and returned to the rectangular
space I share with others of my kind.
We nestle together, edges cradling
edges. I am safe in the closed drawer.

Even the knives sleep.

"It's nine o'clock," Dianne says.

"But *you* haven't read," says Liz.

"All right, if you insist. Here's my dialogue with Spinoza. He believed that everything is interconnected. That everything is everything."

"Take *that* oxymorons," Ernest whispers.

* * *

"I really liked this evening," I say to Ernest as we enter his car.

"I did, too," he says.

41

"I like that it was so Columbus. Not New York, Chicago or San Francisco. Just simple, easy, grounded. Friendly. Unpretentious."

"We should come again," Ernest says.

"I really like the bookstore, too. I'll see if they want my old books."

"Give them to them. Keep the store in business."

"Great idea."

* * *

Somewhat more than seven minutes later, Ernest and I are home and settled on our kitchen chairs. "So, tell me about Keats's poem," I say. "*Seeing Chapman's Homer for the first time.* Did he see a bust of Homer?"

"Chapman's Homer," Ernest says gently correcting me "is Chapman's *translation* of Homer."

Ernest talks about the poem. Although Keats had read much poetry ("realms of gold"), and had read translations of Homer before, he had never "got" how great a bard Homer was until he read Chapman's translation. Reading it, Keats felt like Cortez—the *second* European traveler to the Pacific Ocean (after Balboa). Cortez returns to tell of his voyage of discovery, just as Keats tell us of his, inviting us to experience second-hand the "loud and bold" resolve into "silent awe."

"Ah," I say. "I get it. And I get why Liz had us do the oxymoron exercise, too! *Loud...silent.*"

Ernest smiles. He has been retired for four years from teaching English and has probably not read Keats's poem for over thirty years, or even thought of it, but it comes back to him immediately. Now, when he recites it—commonsense and structure—I understand it.

"And what about that oxymoronic writing you put into your pocket?" I ask.

"Oh, this little thing?" Ernest says, taking out the slip of paper. He reads:

> Oh, Sweet—
> I'm nearly tight enough
> To recall
> Without bitterness
> The civil war
> In our slacks.

"You wrote a poem!"

"It is ours. And, we're still writing it."

On the wall behind us is the sampler I made fifteen years ago. On it, I had cross-stitched Samuel Johnson's aphorism about second marriages: *The Triumph of Hope Over Experience.*

HOME ALONE

It has been over a year since I have been home alone, and I'm hungry for it. Ernest will be gone for five days and four nights. I intend to use my time alone wisely. I'll have no interruptions or obligations, save a potluck brunch with my new book club and an afternoon with my grandson, Akiva.

On the first day, I fritter. I write reference letters for ex-students, order library books, phone Betty, phone Melli, sniffle, walk about the neighborhood, nap, twice, whimper, cry for no reason that I know of, and eat pb & j sandwiches for breakfast, lunch and dinner. I mess with a personal essay that needs to be left alone. *But shouldn't that be a semi-colon?* I tinker more seriously with its cover letter which grows from two paragraphs to four and shrinks back to three. I can't stop fussing. I know where I want to submit the essay but I can't seem to let it go.

What's the big deal? I ask myself. *It's only an essay.* But it is more than that. After three long years of waffling, this year I am determined to make the transition in identity from *university professor* to *writer.* This Personal Essay is my definitive first move. And that's a big deal.

I've made submitting the essay an even bigger deal by reading too many books about creative non-fiction, as if figuring it all out, as an academic might, will get me somewhere different. "More! Quicker!"—as the university's provost wrote on the vita of a blind faculty member, denying her promotion.

I mess some more with my cover letter.

Nine p.m. and time to watch my Highlights of the Olympics video to be enchanted again by the ice-skating pair dancers. At 11:30 I print the Personal Essay and its cover letter and stick them in a manila envelope, which I don't seal. To relax a little, I play some Free Cell. At 2:30 a.m., too relaxed to sleep and remembering the potluck brunch the next day, I take kava-kava and set the alarm.

That night, I dream the Olympic Figure Skating judges are judging me. Perched on their high-rise podium behind a long table with laptops and pencils, scowling their supercilious scowls, they judge me. My score is "*You need a husband.*"

* * *

Apparently, I forgot to push the switch on the alarm clock because it does not go off. When I do wake up, I have 45 minutes to get ready and get where I'm going, although I'm not sure where that is because I didn't find out last night when I was at the computer playing Free Cell.

I don't take a shower. I don't even take off my sleeping socks. I leave my toothbrush, paste and deodorant on the bathroom counter, my pajamas on the bathroom floor. Seeing that my clothes from yesterday are blessedly not on hangers but peeking out from under the comforter, I go for them. Spying dressy shoes by the dresser, I imagine a new Olympic sport—Speed Dressing—me, ready in a slung from the shoulder black dress, bed socks, slip-on shoes and earrings on wires.

Coming down the stairs, I curse myself for not having, last night, set up the coffee pot, measured out my Metamucil, and collected my five prescriptions and seven vitamins into their small crystal bowl.

Yikes! I have to make my famous spinach salad. I work fast. Left behind on one counter and on the floor are apple peelings, spinach leaves, walnut bits; on another counter are the makings of the dressing, walnut oil, olive oil, lemon juice, rice vinegar, maple syrup. A burnt piece of Stan Evans rye remains half-popped up in the toaster, next to the Jiff and Smucker's jars, empty, I notice, The sink holds dirty dishes, including yesterday's table knives, today's cutting board and the MOMA ice-cream dipper, resting in chocolatey water in the bowl from last night's Olympic sundae, three heavenly dips of Graeter's vanilla soaked in Hershey's syrup. Beside the bowl is the empty Cheez-it box, the contents of which Maxwell the Cat and I consumed, stretched out together on the couch.

The good news is that I forgot to turn off the computer last night so I can quickly retrieve the needed phone number and address. I call. I'll be ten minutes late which violates my self-image as an on-time kind of gal.

* * *

This brunch is the first meeting of my new book club. We're getting to know one another at a member's house. Annie says if anyone wants any ironing done, she's their girl. "I do," I say, thinking of the king-sized cotton duvet wadded up in Ernest's dresser drawer. I had spent five or six nights ironing it a month or so ago; now, it's been washed and is a crumpled mess again. I'm sure not going to iron it.

Stephanie says she loves to proof read. "Will you proof read for me?" I ask, thinking of the essay whose fate is yet to be sealed. Shirley says she loves to teach chanting. "Oh, teach me," I say. I can't think of anything I can do for anyone.

"I'm a good task-master," I say, finally honing in on my one useful skill. "Let's decide how often we are going to meet."

* * *

After brunch, we head to Border's Bookstore for the actual book club meeting. Since my house is on the way, I decide to stop and get the duvet. I almost trip over the recycling bin that I had brought back inside after the recyclers had emptied it and that I had not yet brought down to the basement. It's convenient here in the kitchen, though, because I can just put the newspaper sections into the bin as I finish them.

"There's a lot of newspaper yet to read or not," I say out loud to myself. "The table is a total mess…Oh, well."

I step over my Nikes, pause to take another chocolate cream from the Anthony Thomas candy Ernest gave me. They're about half gone. "Hmm. Did I eat all of those last night?" I question myself out loud as I head up the stairs.

"Just look at this bedroom! Bed unmade. Laundry not put away. Piles of pillows on the floor and hope chest. Dirty clothes on the floor. Shoes everywhere. Let's see! One, two, three, four, five pairs! Six dresser drawers open! Panty hose hanging out! *Is that my mother talking*? No, it's me talking to myself out-loud. Ah, there's the duvet, just where I left it," I triumphantly announce to the room.

"Let's see. A big plastic bag would hold this duvet but wait a minute. There's an empty mailing box that I haven't taken outside to the trash. I'll use that."

As long as I'm home, I think, I might as well check the answering machine. Maybe Ernest will have phoned.

"Hello, Laurel," the disembodied voice says. "This is Bee. It's 12:45. Did we agree that I was coming to clean today while Ernest was away?"

"Oh my God, I hope not!"

"…just to keep you in shape. Are you ready for me? Are things put away? I have a terrible headache so if I don't hear from you, I won't come."

"Thank God," I say, turning my back on the empty glasses and scribbled notes surrounding the answering machine. Bee's business is called *Cleanliness Next*. She has a religious calling to help the deserving cleaning-impaired. To be "deserving" one must declutter counters and straighten up the house before she arrives. She almost fired us once. "Her clients," she told us, "do not leave dirty dishes in the sink."

"Not today, Bee. Not ready!" I speak into the air.

* * *

"Annie, I brought the duvet," I say as we walk towards our cars after our book club meeting. Annie looks stunned. *Oh my, maybe she didn't mean it. Maybe she doesn't want to iron. I took her at her word.* "I'll pay of course."

"…I can't do it today…" Annie stammers.

"…and if you find it's too big to do, then don't of course…and no, I wouldn't expect it before next month, at the earliest…take your time."

"Is it *in* something?"

"…here, in this box…crumpled."

This feels so awkward. Will we be able to be friends, if she does my ironing? Is she like Bee? Should I have straightened the duvet before I gave it to her? Well, at least I resisted emailing my Personal Essay to Stephanie for proofreading. *But, maybe I can still do that.*

I come home exhausted. Duvet-less. I sort the mail, throwing most of mine into the now conveniently located recycling bin. I put Ernest's mail neatly on his desk with *The New Yorker, The Atlantic* and flyers on the bottom and bills on the top. Naptime.

* * *

The next nights and days are like the first ones, except there is no scheduled brunch. The house gets progressively messier; my sleep progressively more erratic; my Free Cell skills progressively stronger. On the fourth afternoon, I pick-up my grandson, Akiva. He is three and a half.

"Grampa has gone to California," I tell him. "I'll be alone for five days."

"Only four."

"Four nights, honey, but five days."

"Only four," he insists, "because I am here today."

For the afternoon, I am his Queen and he is my Knight in shining armor, fighting off all invaders, conquering all challenges.

"Queen, what do I need to take care of?" he asks, as I put the faux gold crown upon my head and he wiggles into his armor.

"In my bedroom," I say, "there is an infestation of dragonettes."

He wields his sword and blowpipe, dispelling the invaders, while I hang up clothes, put away shoes, close drawers, and make the bed.

"What else?" he asks.

"In the kitchen there are hemi-lizards," I answer regally as I clear up the counters, sink and table-top.

With great majesty Sir Akiva rids the entire house of its goblins, gargoyles, and all manner of malicious intruders.

"Any other challenges?" he asks.

"Well, there is this Important Message that must needs be taken to Town Square for the Runner to take to the Mystical Land of Chicago," I say, removing my crown, "but I lack the resolve."

"Where's the 'portent message?"

"Here. In this brown envelope."

Licking the edge, Akiva says, "There. I have sealed it with dragon juice. I'll bring my sword and protect you and resolve you."

* * *

This is now the morning of the fifth day. My essay is in the mail and my house is straightened up. Last night, I dreamt I was ice-skate dancing with Ernest who said I was as light on my skates as I was a light to his eyes. He loved my glitteriness. There were no judges. When I wake up, I leave a note on top of his mail: Welcome Home!

SIMPLY WHITE

Eighteen years have passed since we moved to Revere Street and replaced the yellows and avocado-greens of the small Cape Cod with blues and browns and flowered wallpaper, drapes and sconces. I am so ready for another change. I want everything painted simply white. Everything. And I want all the bathroom fixtures and kitchen appliances and even the washing machine and dryer pristine white. I know I cannot bring back the large house I left in Clintonville with its white walls, but I can delete color and create whiteness.

My Columbus family is here to help Ernest and me get this done.

"Let's get this wood paneling down right now!" I declare. I am so done with it.

"Hand me the crowbar," Josh says to Ben.

Fifteen minutes later the paneling is off the wall. Tami and Ben have removed the nails and carried the debris to the outside trash can.

We stand back and admire the dry wall.

"Look here," Ernest says to four-year old Akiva. "What do you think?"

"We're good archeologists," my granddaughter Shana, says. "A different tribe lived here and has left its mark!"

On the drywall, we see:

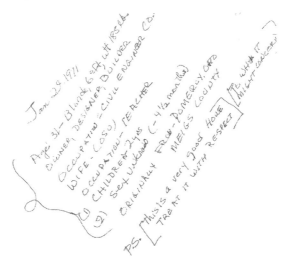

51

"I think our tribe should leave our mark, too," I say. "Everyone—here—grab a pencil."

"Izit okay to write on Gramma's wall?" Akiva asks.

"Yes."

Our tribe gets to it!

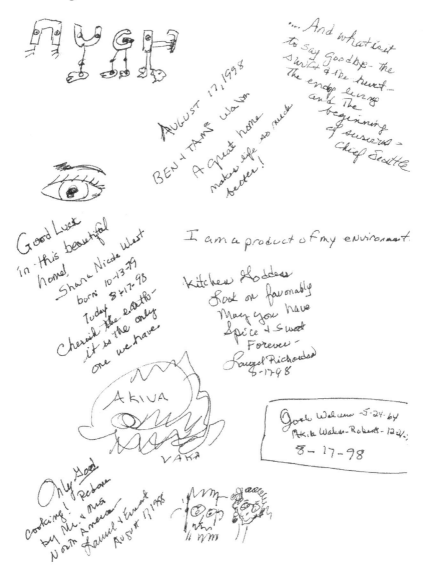

The next day both tribes' contributions to the archeological history of Weybridge are painted over with Benjamin Moore's *Simply White* paint but not before I have taken pictures of our tribe's presence.

* * *

I walk around the rooms of my house, most now painted simply white like the rooms were in my Clintonville house, university district duplex and in all the apartments I had lived in after I left my parents' home. If I thought making everything white might recapture my youth somehow—or slow down the annoying and inevitable changes in my skin and bones—I was wrong. What it did was make the house feel more like my home.

* * *

I prepare a dinner homage to my Jewish mother and Irish father. Grammas's porcelain inlaid copper serving dish brought by her from Kiev in 1908 is washed and polished.

I cover the old oak table with a white table-cloth, crocheted by my mother and given to me on my thirteenth birthday for my "hope chest." A most disappointing present, then, but a sweet memory, now. I place six crystal salters, a wedding gift from my sister Jessica on the table. I set it with the gold trimmed plates and gold silverware my attorney father's client, Al Capone, had given to my parents as a wedding gift, and which my mother had given to me when she and Dad moved to Florida. When the time comes, I will give them to my sons and they to their children. Or, so I like to think.

I never thought that perhaps the dinnerware and goldware were purchased with monies illegally earned or with human travail and suffering. "Al," my father had told me, "never killed a woman or child or any man outside the crime families. He refused to take part in the drug syndicates. He knew drugs would endanger teenagers." When I looked dubious, Father would continue, "Back in the day in Chicago, Al was considered a modern day Robin Hood. He stole from the rich and opened soup kitchens…he paid politicians and got milk bottles dated so kids would be safe…and every day he went to City Hall to lobby for something good for the people of Chicago."

I liked listening to my father white-wash Al Capone.

* * *

"Dinner's ready," I say. "Come and get it!"

"Smells diff'rent," says Akiva, sniffing. His mother is a vegan. "Smells good."

"Yes…It's *kosher* corned-beef and cabbage."

"I jes'll eat cabbage," Akiva declares. "I like white food."

"Mmm," hum Josh and Ben.

NEW YEAR'S EVE

"Let's hope that ball in Times Square is the only thing that crashes at midnight," retired mathematician Joe says. He is the kindest of men. It is five o'clock. Ten neighbors gather at Bob and Martha's for their annual New Year Eve's party. This is the only time when we are all together under the same roof. I chat with my neighbors when I see them, but mostly Ernest and I keep to ourselves. We are older and uninterested in happy hours. I rarely know about the problems our neighbors confront while they are confronting them but I get a catch-up at the New Year's Eve party.

When I lived in Clintonville, neighbors with emotional needs would drop-in, talk, cry and not leave. I worked at home a lot—and still do. I am a good and practiced listener. Those neighbors' needs for companionship, tea and sympathy, intruded on my need for time. With a professor's job and two sons, time was precious. And, because I turned to friends—not neighbors—for support, the neighborly relationships that developed were imbalanced, unequal in vulnerability.

I feel fortunate that my Revere Street neighbors do not drop-in but do look-out for my house when we are gone. When we return, the house is still standing, neither burnt nor burgled. There are no pesky brochures littering our porch or strangling our door knob. Our trash cans are back behind their fence, our front lawn mowed. I would never hesitate to ask Bob, who is fifteen years younger than I am, to help me with something heavy or hard—like getting my car out of the garage. There is something inexplicably reassuring about this latent dependence.

We have Bob and Martha over for a fancy dinner once a year to thank them. I keep thinking about having a party for all the neighbors but I never do. Mostly because we don't serve alcohol. Maybe as they age, alcohol will be less important to them and I can have that party. I like the non-intimate intimacy and predictability of being with these neighbors on New Year's Eve. Whatever differences we might have in politics and religion are irrelevant as we all seem to share the same values or at least act as if we do. No one breaches that sense of camaraderie. Everyone is nice. I like them all.

"This could be the end of the world as we know it," mathematician Joe says, stroking his gray beard. He pours himself a hefty glass of white wine.

"The government is prepared," Bob says, pouring himself a generous glass of red.

"Yeah," says salesman Max, pouring a copious second glass of red. "Sure. Like we can trust any program called…What is it called, again?"

"The Information and Redress Disclosures Act," Ernest, who knows everything, says. "Or something like that." He pours himself a huge glass of Diet Coke.

"No," says scientist Martha, looking up from her kitchen sink where she is cutting veggies. "That program is silly. The one I'm counting on is the Infrastructure Protection Group."

"Scaremongering," says lawyer Dale emptying his glass of red. "It's all about the media creating crises so that you'll watch more television and they can sell more ads so the capitalists can sell more useless stuff to Dumbos. Do you know companies are selling high-stakes security systems and insurance policies?"

"Hey, there Dale," Max interrupts. "I'm selling those policies." Max opens a new bottle of red.

"There could be a lot of legal issues," Dale's stay-at-home wife, Nora, says. She helps herself to white.

"You can't sue the Federal Government, Nora," Dale counters.

"If the infrastructure goes," our hostess Martha continues her thought, "that means street-lights, electricity, phones, heat, water. Airplanes… God…"

"Well, let's look on the bright-side," says pre-school teacher Annabelle. She pours a little red into her glass, twirls and sniffs it. "Maybe I won't have to teach anymore!!"

"Retire, already, Annabelle. Retire!" Ernest says. "You're burnt out." Ernest has already been retired from his professorship for eight years. He was burnt out at 52.

"Well, one good thing is all the extra work for soft-ware engineers," I interject. I'm thinking of all the comp time my son Ben has racked up.

"Those jerks!" Bob proclaims. "Throughout the computer industry, the so-called soft-ware engineers programmed only two digits for coding a year. For the new millennium we need four digits." He chomps on a carrot-stick. "What jerks!"

"Maybe they thought the world was going to end," wide-eyed Annabelle offers.

"Do you know why it's called Y2K?" Joe bangs the table. "Listen up," he says as if we are students in an Algebra class. "Y stands for *year*. And K stands for *kilo*." He can hardly contain his excitement, "A kilo is a thousand so 2K is two-thousand. The Year Two Thousand. Get it?" His face looks like a red balloon ready to burst.

"Thanks, Joe," I say. I love his enthusiastic altruism. He misses teaching.

"I'm concerned about Y2K as a human problem," endocrinologist Rhonda says, sipping on her home-made veggie drink. "People are hoarding food, buying cans of crap they'll never want to eat. Banks are running out of cash. My patients are filling their bathtubs with water. They've filled their prescriptions in advance and loaded up on antibiotic creams and band-aids. They're scared. They think there will be a lot of looting and killing."

"Well, I'm a born Democrat," Bob says, "but I've got my 45 loaded."

"Great, Bob," says Martha. I can't tell if she means it.

"What concerns me," says Joe, "is what's going to happen to all those medical devices with chips in them that we have in our homes."

"My Bi-Pap?" Ernest shakes his head. "Crashing?"

"Can I sell any of you an analog clock?" Max asks.

"Help yourself," Martha says, signaling the official start of the potluck.

Each year Ernest and I bring stuffed grape-leaves and each year I am asked if I made them. "No," I always say. Rhonda always brings six or seven different kinds of organic, sugar-free cookies. She makes them herself. Others bring cheese, wine, crackers, wine, salads, wine, meatballs. Bob and Martha always provide Diet Coke.

* * *

"Ready?" Bob asks, signaling us into the family room. On a very large table is his collection of small spring-driven mechanical toys. When Bob was growing-up he played with his father's collection on New Year's Eve. Bob inherited them, added to them, and has continued the tradition. Only on New Year's Eve are the toys out to play. Over the years, Ernest and I have added to the collection, usually with some dorky toy I find in unlikely places, like museum shops.

The party circles the table. The clickety-click of keys turning springs is music to my ears. Soon, Captain Marvel attacks a dinosaur. A Chevy pick-up battles a robot with blinking eyes. Pink Panther, moving in an ever increasing circular motion, falls off the table. An oversized crawling baby takes on the lion-tamer, whose lion is sitting on its haunches. The Boy-Bear-Band musicians play on—drumming, strumming, blowing, tooting, clanging.

"My caterpillar can outdistance yours," Annabelle says, challenging Dale to a duel.

"You're on!" Dale says.

"Lanes" are cleared and the two caterpillars inch themselves across the table.

"A gold star for trying, Dale," Annabelle says, triumphantly stroking her winning caterpillar.

"The oscillating toys are my favorite," says Joe, who winds up a circus clown and watches it go back and forth in a circle. "I think Euler had a formula to predict…"

"Hey," I say, "Watch my duck waddle."

"Look out duckie," says Ernest, "here comes a man with a long-shot-gun."

"This looks like a rescued dog," Joe says, petting a black plastic puppy. He winds it up and watches it go back and forth in a straight line. "Hmnm… Reciprocal motion."

"And its tail wags!" Nora says.

"You need some women action figures," Rhonda says, winding-up Batman.

"Hard to find them," Martha says, winding up Robin. The two do a pas de deux.

"I challenge all of you!" Max says. "Who will be the fastest?"

"We'll all need linear moving toys," Joe instructs us. "I mean I'm telling you this just so the playing field will be fair. You need a wind-up that just goes straight ahead. Period. No arcs or parabolas. Now as to the size and weight…"

"I think we can handle this," Max says.

"Ready, set, go!" Bob declares. "And they are off…"

* * *

Ten o'clock and all the neighbors are in their coats, hats and boots with leftovers in their hands. *Great to see you…thanks…turn your heat up high tonight… fill your tubs…get out your flashlights…Happy New Year…*

* * *

"I'm going to call Ben and Josh and wish them happy New Year," I say to Ernest.

"Good idea. I'll call my daughters."

"Do you want to stay up and watch that ball fall in New York's Times Square?"

"Wouldn't miss it for the world."

NEW YEAR, NEW CENTURY, NEW MILLENIAL

On New Year's morning, I make coffee, turn on my computer,
and take a hot shower.

Everything I need is here.

This New Year, New Centennial, New Millennial will be my only one.

Carpe diem!

I will stay home and be grateful for the people and places in my life.

Tempus Fugit!

How delicious it is to not make a list of resolutions.
How great that my printer works!

The Day after Yesterday
is the only day there is

for us still in bodies.

The Day before tomorrow

is the only day there is.

I am here.

INTERSECTING WORLDS
2001–2003

The optimist thinks this is the best of all worlds;
and the pessimist knows it.

– J. Robert Oppenheimer

OUR SMALL WORLD

I don't like to shower when I am home alone and even when someone else is in the house I'm in and out of the shower as quickly as possible. I thought this was just one of my quirks—a way not to waste energy, time, precious skin oils. But it is not a quirk. Rather my shower aversion, I am realizing, is how my unconscious deals with learning about horrors I was too young to understand.

When I was six, a visitor came to my Sunday School class at Anshe Emet Synagogue in Chicago. She spoke with an odd accent, heavy, fast and angry. I try to listen but I am not sure I understand her.

"Jewish boys and girls just like you," she tells us, "are having their skins made into lampshades." I think the children would look weird and be very cold without their skins.

"Nazi doctors are experimenting on children. They break their bones and set them wrong."

My Christian Scientist trained father would not let my broken arm get fixed and it healed wrong. A doctor broke it again and set it right. But why would doctors set broken bones wrong on purpose? Are the Nazi doctors against medicine, like my father?

"Nazi doctors give Jewish children diseases and make them sick."

My mother put me in bed with my brother Barrie when he had measles and again when he had chicken pox so I would get them and be sick, too. Is my mother a Nazi?

"Jewish men and women are separated at the camp. Men go into one room and women into another to get naked. They are brought together again to the showers. But the showers have gas in them that kills all the Jewish men and women."

On a very hot July day that summer, my parents drop Barrie and me off at a large public pool. I have never been to a public pool before. My brother and I are separated. A woman dressed in a gray uniform tells me to get naked. She looks me over, puts my clothes in a wire basket, gives me a key, and tells me to get my suit on and go to the showers. I have never been in a shower before, never even seen one. Water is coming from the ceiling

65

and the walls. I run through the showers into a narrow passage. The passage floor is ankle high in a strong smelling green liquid. I run out to the pool. A different gray uniformed woman puts me into a metal bin where purple light streams over me. I try to run away. I collapse.

"She's had a heat-stroke," I hear a woman say.

"Are her parents here?" a man asks.

"We've not located them."

I don't know what a heat stroke is and I don't know if the green light and purple light have taken off my skin or whether or not my parents sent me to the showers or whether they are in the showers, too. I see my brother. I want to sleep.

* * *

These are the memories I was writing on the Eve of September 11th, 2001. It is the beginning of a longer work on how knowledge of trauma begets trauma; how innocence is lost; how vulnerable are the children. Learning at such a young age about horrors against children and families deeply affects one's life. My life—from showers to politics to friendships to arenas I have yet to explore—has been constructed to avoid and/or control the unfathomable.

When I hear of the airplanes and the towers, my first thought is the children. Oh, the lives of the children! What is happening? What will children be told? What will they understand? And then I see that the children are seeing what the adults are seeing on television and hearing what adults are hearing. The children are seeing the airplane, and the second tower, and the airplane/tower, airplane/tower over and over again until All Fall Down. And All Fall Down again and again.

My heart breaks for the children whose lives are broken and I am thinking about every child. Our Global Village. Our Small World.

* * *

My list serves are repositories for quick fixes, ideological purity, self-blame. I can't join the discussion. I refuse to intellectualize, analyze or academize. I don't have any answers. I am not even sure what the questions are.

* * *

Ernest's jazz band is riffing in our dining room. I hear the vocalist, a member of an international peace committee, say, "Everyone is signing the international human rights petition, but secretly they are not convinced." *Let's fall in Love*, she sings. And the band plays on.

I call my friend Marilyn, a hospice volunteer. That's where she was when she saw the towers go down. She cried. Then went into a patient's room to change his sheets. My friend was chastised for not "seeing the big picture, tending to small stuff." I call my best friend Betty. She says the children she sees on television are of one accord: *Are airplanes safe*? I call my step-daughter, back from her family's missionary work in Russia. Her daughters, Nadia and Katie, are having nightmares. I call Akiva's mother. Akiva is afraid an airplane will hit his school because it is a big building. Akiva and his friend Olivia are the only two children in his class who have not seen the airplanes/towers on television. But they know about it.

* * *

My feminist-postmodernist theory group meets a week after the Towers. We are stressed. One member says she is suffering from "ideological dislocation." She doesn't know what to think. She doesn't know what is right. Opposing Viet Nam was clear. But now? I suggest that this is an *open moment*, a time when we are confused, uncertain. The attack and the human rights violations are abhorrent but we don't like war. We begin to talk about *just* wars. When can a war be just? When might the refusal to engage create a worsened world? More deaths? Ignoring Churchill's dire warnings prior to 1939 when Hitler invaded Poland led to 50 million deaths in Germany, Poland, Austria, France, England, Russia—and to the atom bomb, Hiroshima and Nagasaki. And to untold numbers of traumatized children, like me.

* * *

On the following Sunday, a Unitarian minister sermonizes about the Taliban. "They hate us," he says, "because we are exporting American culture." He suggests that instead of "dropping missiles, we should drop Teddy Bears on the people of Afghanistan." *Is he serious*? I think he is. Does he not know that the Teddy Bear is an American icon named after the Rough Rider president, Theodore Roosevelt? It is a symbol of American expansionism at any cost. I notice that the congregants are nodding their heads in agreement with the minister. Maybe they'll take up a collection to buy the Teddy Bears? *Where am I?* The place where I have found simpatico friends, solace and comfort is offering me none of these. I leave the Church in anger and despair. I send "thinking of you" cards to ten friends in other cities.

* * *

Seven of us gather for coffee at The Village Café. We all claim to be committed to open discussion, justice, and diversity of opinions.

"Violence is always wrong," says one of my favorite people.

"I don't know," I say. "I just don't know."

The silence is palpable.

"Violence is always objectionable," another says.

"Do you object to America's involvement in World War II?" I ask.

"I was too young," he stammers.

"What do you think?" I ask Rosa, a Polish Catholic who was in a concentration camp.

"Violence is always wrong," she says.

Does she not know that she would not be here today if Allies had not engaged Hitler? Or, is she side-stepping the question? Saying what she thinks others want to hear? I feel disconnected, unable to read my friends.

* * *

Email from a friend: "What is all this talk about being opposed to war? Don't people know that World War III has already begun?"

* * *

Some of my best friends are liberal; some are conservative. None of them *want* war. They differ on their evaluation of war as a right or wrong action on moral, economic, and strategic grounds. I feel as if I am living in a civil war where families and friends are deeply divided. My dreams are about death and destruction. In one, I am a badly wrapped mummy. "Fear" and "Anxiety" attend me. I practice "cerebral hygiene." No television news, no newspaper news, no radio news hours, no magazines; no list serves. I avoid public events. All media. I avoid topics. "Do you feel constrained in your speech?" my naturopath asks me, dispensing homeopathic drugs for my throat chakra.

* * *

I call Betty. "I am very stressed," I tell her. "I don't know what's right or wrong. Worse, I don't know how to know. We just don't know what's going on in the hearts and minds of world leaders. You know, I feel very lonely. I can't enter conversations. I can't pick up on the discourses. What gets me through the day is believing that people of good will have different analyses."

She snaps back, "I don't believe that."

* * *

My granddaughter Shana has plans to teach English in Hiroshima. Despite her somewhat cynical bumper-sticker—"Whirled Peas"—she desperately wants *world peace*. Shana is very taken with the mayor of Hiroshima's peace messages. I wonder if I should share with her Elie Wiesel memoir. *Even with my own granddaughter, I am unsure what to say.* In 1987, the holocaust survivor, Wiesel met in Hiroshima with high-ranking Japanese officials. "I shall never forget Hiroshima," he said, "but you must never forget Pearl Harbor." The officials were "unsettled" by his remarks.

* * *

I go to a lecture billed as conciliation between Christians, Jews and Muslims. The lecturer talks about a time, during the Caliphate, when everyone lived in peace. "A few Christians," he said, "were beheaded, which was inevitable because they were questioning the Prophet Mohammed. They should have known better. Fortunately, the remaining Christians were more sensible." The lecturer does not mention the fate of Jews.

* * *

"The Jewish Body and Anti-Semitism," is the title of the Sunday morning lecture at Beth Tikvah. The lecturer talks about how caricatures of Jewish people are interwoven with anti-Semitism starting with the middle ages when Jews were drawn as satanic creatures with cloven feet, horns, tails. I think about my ex-husband's mother, a Protestant from the small town of Port Orchard, Washington. She had never seen a Jew before. "Do you mind if I feel your horns?" she asked, touching my head.

"The Middle-Ages believed that Jews were emissaries of the devil," the lecturer continues. "The Jews were accused of ritually reenacting the crucifixion by kidnapping and killing Christian children and using their blood to make Passover food." I am thinking I am thankful we are past the Middle-Ages.

"Nazis revived these accusations," the lecturer says. "And they are taught, today, to children in some middle-east countries. The hoax book—*Protocols of the Elders of Zion*—is taught as if it were a true and factual book of Jewish intent to take over the world." *What world are they talking about?*

When I leave the lecture, the halls of the Synagogue are filled with exuberant little children coming out of their Sunday School classes. Some are Asian; some African-American; some African; some have red hair and freckles; and some have eyes as bright as candles, lit for Shabbat.

When I see these little Jewish children, I want to touch them and hug them. Smile at them with joy.

"Here's the future," I say to a teacher.

"May they have one," she says.

* * *

Peace-Activists are set-up by a church near me. One of their signs says, "Honk, if you want peace." I honk. *Who doesn't want peace?* But, what is the best course for a *lasting* peace? I don't know. All the name-calling just doesn't help. I just don't know—

* * *

My grandson Akiva transfers to a smaller school where he feels safer. Nadia and Katie back from Russia emulate the PowerPuff Girls. They fight evil.

I send money to a newly opened Hebrew pre-school in Kiev. I seem to talk less and less to my friends. I wonder if I have reached a place where what I think about exceeds the boundaries of the theories I have embraced. I turn back to my writing. I read the newspaper, again: Iraq, North Korea, Senegal, Israel, Palestine, Lebanon, Syria, Zimbabwe, Pakistan, Thailand, Cyprus, Venezuela, Uganda. The World. Everywhere. Our Small World.

WHAT IS BLACK & WHITE & RED ALL OVER?

The newspaper
says that
twelve years
after the
black ash
white light
red sky
our economy
will be back
to normal.

MEMORIAL DAY PARADE

Let it be known that he who wears the Military Order
of the Purple Heart has given of his blood in the
defense of his homeland and shall forever be
revered by his fellow countrymen.

– President George Washington

As I near the corner of Revere Street and High, I hear a marching band playing *America the Beautiful.* I sing along, "...from sea to shining sea." I am crying. For the music? For my love of America? For my fear for Her?

I reach the corner in time to applaud the soldiers from World War II. They are riding in an open military truck that might have served time in Germany. The soldiers are few and old. One has a Purple Heart medal. My tears increase. German soldiers had lined up my Russian Jewish extended family with all the other Jews of Kiev, shot them and laughed as they fell into the ravine at Babi Yar. Had my grandmother not brought my mother to America to escape the 1908 pogroms, they too would have died at Babi Yar. I would not be here. I remind myself of this often. If we had lost the war to Germany, I would not be here, either. I am overwhelmed with gratitude for the soldiers in this truck coming down High Street, soldiers who risked their lives and saved mine.

I applaud the next military truck carrying even fewer men. They look bent and beaten. They are the Korean War Veterans. My brother-in-law John could be in their truck. He was a Marine sergeant on Pork Chop Hill, the only member of his platoon to survive. He has never overcome his post-traumatic stress. He drives fearlessly through flooded intersections yelling, "Oh, so you think you can stop me!" "Take that!" he yells, gunning his motor, skirting around a car going the speed limit and then braking in front of it. Once, when I was in the passenger seat, I tightened my grip on the door-handle and "braked" with my right foot. "Afraid, are you? Get Out!" he yelled. "And you, too," he said to my sister Jessica in the back seat. We were in the middle of a freeway. He slammed on the brakes and we got out. My heart sobs for John and these other irreparable Korean War Veterans riding in the beaten-up truck.

A young man passes out little American flags. I thank him.

To my right, I notice a woman in a bright yellow shirt standing on the curb. She's holding up a large yellow sign: "Peace be unto you." I think about it. Does she mean that these soldiers should know peace because of what they have sacrificed? Or does she mean that they never should have been soldiers to begin with but that they are "forgiven"? Or could be forgiven if they got their religious beliefs right?

I notice another woman in bright yellow sitting on a fold-up chair. She is heavy-set. The P.O.W. truck is approaching us. She stands, walks into the street, and raises her yellow sign above her head, twisting it so the men in the truck can read it: "Study War No More."

"Your sign is rude," I say to the woman as I step in front of the sign.

"It's a free country," she says.

"*Still,*" I say "Guess why?"

She sits back down. I stay standing in front of her.

A truck honoring the Missing-in Action approaches. Women and children are in this truck. I think of my ex-husband's uncle, a jet pilot, who went missing over Japan in 1945, and how his wife never lost faith that he would be found. Even having his body would be better than this living in limbo, she had thought. I wave my little American flag.

The heavy-set woman gets up, circumvents me and goes into the street, hoisting her "Study War No More" sign overhead. It looks like she might walk in front of the M.I.A. truck, forcing it to stop, but she backs off.

"Your sign is so rude," I repeat, as she returns to her chair.

"It's in the Bible," she says. Righteousness is pouring out of her with every syllable.

"Not in my Bible," I retort.

"She can protest the protest!" a skinny man in yellow says.

"This is not a protest," I say. "It's a memorial service!"

"I have my rights," she yells.

"*Still,*" I say. "Still…"

"Don't start with me," she threatens. She makes a fist and glares at me.

"Peace and Love?" I say, handing her my little American flag.

Have I been threatened? Has she?

I walk on, watch the approaching parade, and scan the side-walks. I don't see any more yellow signs.

The Weybridge Community Band is playing "Stars and Stripes forever." I hope so.

CHEZ PROVENCE

Today is one of those surprisingly wonderful early June days in Ohio, sunny, but not humid, sailor blue skies, a slight breeze and all manner of trees in full leaf, impatiens spilling out of window boxes and orange daylilies spilling on the sidewalks, kissing my calves as I pass by, sauntering on my quarter-mile walk to Chez Provence, a bistro and bakery built around a vintage oven imported from France.

A dozen tables snuggle beneath red and white unfurled umbrellas on the brick patio behind a jardin wall. Inside Chez Provence two rooms have stone fireplaces and a third holds the yawing mouth of the oven, the food line and the bakery. In every room, D-Day is memorialized with photos and commendations. The scent of baguettes and the sound of French street music fills the air, inside and outside the restaurant.

Opened three years ago, Chez Provence has become a Weybridge favorite for couples, families and "women who lunch." I am one of those. Today I am having lunch with Bryn, a member of Women's Poetry Workshop. Bryn has arrived early and is securing "our" table in the shade in the far corner of the patio. She's wearing her signature khaki colored tailored clothes. Her hairline is receding from the weight of her ponytail, secured by a rubber band as it probably has been her entire life.

Bryn and I have odd and deep connections. We were both married to academics and because of them we had come to Columbus; we both divorced and raised two sons, mostly on our own; we secured our own tenure track positions in the social sciences; we wrote feminist poetry; and we served on university committees dedicated to helping women. I finally decided that the committees were a ruse, a way the university could claim they were doing something when they weren't. Bryn never lost hope, though, that the next committee might be the one that would make a difference. I felt sorry for her about doing all that scut-work for nothing, but that was not how she parsed it. She saw "soldiering on," as she put it, as a way of giving homage to her Army father. She would fight to the bitter end. She would never give up.

Bryn and I leave a book, a tote bag and sweater on our table to hold it while we go inside and get in line for our lunches. We never worry that the stuff might be stolen. This is Weybridge. This is Chez Provence! We worry only that we might lose our table.

Inside, one young man is manning the food line and the bakery line, both of which are growing longer the longer we wait. In the front of the food line, a husband, wife and child are trying to decide what they want and whether they want to eat-in or take-away. As one makes up her/his mind, another changes his/hers. Life in their house must be a place of serious indecision. I am having trouble making up my mind, too.

"Bon appétit," the young man says to the family as they pick up their take-away choices. "Excuse'm moi," he says to the next people in line, two eightyish women, dressed in matching Blair catalogue outfits. One of them has a back-curve, a cane and watery blue eyes. They've been studying the menu board, making and unmaking their minds up, too.

The young man steps away from the food line to the bakery line. "May I help you?" he asks a heavy-set woman. She orders five baguettes, sliced, croissants, a dozen apricot and raspberry tarts to go.

"Is that all for you?" a skinny women in shorts standing behind her asks.

"Don't I wish," the large woman says. Soon the two women are laughing and screeching. I feel as if I am in some kind of warzone; my ears hurt from their rat-a-tat-tat bursts. The young man finishes the order and begins waiting on the rest of the bakery brigade rather than returning to the food line. I cannot keep the annoyed look off my face but Bryn signals me with her index finger to her mouth to keep my mouth shut.

"He's doing the best he can," Bryn says.

"Bonjour, Mesdames," the owner, Marcel, noticing the problem with the service comes out from the kitchen. He smiles at the two older women and asks, "May I help you?"

"Oui," the first old woman says, tentatively. "I'll have tomato basil soup and bread."

"Tomato basil soup, please," the second older woman says. "And bread."

"Café?"

"No," the women half-whisper. The first one takes a ten-dollar bill from her wallet and asks, "Will this be enough?"

"Bon appétit, Mesdames," Marcel says, handing back the money. "In honor of D-Day, you do not have to pay. Your husbands helped save France. No?"

"Oui...murky burr-couley." She coughs a dry cough. She bows her head further until her head and neck look like the handle of the cane she's using.

"Bryn!" Marcel says. "Bryn! Bryn! Have anything and everything in honor of your father...And your friend, too. She can have anything."

Marcel makes us plates of quiche, croquet monsieur, salade and brioche, and more plates of tarts and mousse. He puts these on trays along with empty cups for coffee and empty glasses for cold-drinks. He comes around to the line and kisses Bryn on both cheeks. She blushes.

"What does Marcel know about your father?" I ask when we are settled at our patio table.

She explains that when Marcel opened the restaurant he checked for the names of soldiers from Ohio who had died at Normandy. He made it his business to meet their families and thank them personally. He knows what would have happened if American soldiers hadn't taken part.

During the month of June, he treats anyone he thinks might have been a soldier or in the soldier's family to free food and drink.

Bryn and I settle into the beautiful June day. "It's like being in Paris, isn't it?" I say. "Sitting outdoors in our café, watching all the people walk by." I don my sunglasses.

"It does feel like we're somewhere else," Bryn says. "That feels good." She dons her sunglasses.

I start talking. I list all the horrible difficult terrible no-good things that have gone on this fortnight and how I keep losing things. "I lost the birthday book I made for Betty...and I lost—err-forgot my mother's death day...and I lost...I can't even remember what I've lost...That's it...I'm losing my memory, too."

"I don't think I can take it," Bryn says. She wipes off tears under her sunglasses.

"I am so sorry about Donovan being deployed to Iraq," I say. She had told me about her younger son's platoon.

"It's not that," she says. "It's my friends. My colleagues. They say he's going to be a war-criminal for following orders...I feel so alone...They're calling me a war-mongering muthah..."

"How vicious."

"Well, you know how they say that cancer is related to stress?" She shrugs her shoulders.

"What are you telling me, Bryn?" Eight years ago Bryn had colon cancer. Her doctors chose an aggressive treatment plan—surgery, chemo, radiation.

"It's returned. It's in my liver."

Liver. Body central. I wipe away the tears under my sunglasses.

"You're the only one I'm telling about it, outside my family. I'll have scans and I'll be on an experimental drug." She coughs a dry cough. "You know, the five years following my first diagnosis were my happiest years... Maybe the next five will be even happier."

The sun feels good. We sit for the while.

"Do you want a ride home?" Bryn asks.

"I'll walk," I say. "I want to stop at the post-office." I don't say that I need to be alone, to process my sadness, my sorrow, and my appreciation of her trust. *You don't deserve any of this, Bryn. No one does.* How much longer will I have Bryn in my life? How many more times will we be lunching at Chez Provence? I don't want to lose her.

At the post-office, Denzel is busy weighing and printing postage for a bin-load of envelopes. Each envelope requires a considered response from the customer. Does it need to be registered? First class? Return receipt? I check my impatience and say to myself, *Denzel's doing the best he can.*

Finally finished, Denzel turns to me and asks, "So, what did you bring me today?" We kind of know each other after years of meeting this way, in the middle of the town, in the middle of the day, in the middle of the post office with me often bringing artsy envelopes that have to be hand-stamped.

"No mail art today," I say.

"You're killin' me," he says, making a sad face.

"I just need some stamps. Pretty ones."

Denzel opens his drawer and pulls out a sheet of Bob Hope stamps. "That's all I've got."

"I'll take them and a book of the flag stamps."

I start my walk home. The day lilies are asleep. I take out my Bob Hope stamps. They're not great, but he was. For over fifty years he entertained U.S. troops wherever they were stationed.

"I got you some flag stamps," I say to Ernest when I get home.

"Great."

"Whoops! They're not here. I've lost them."

"Someone will find them," he says. "And be happy."

THE DAIRY QUEEN

The Dairy Queen Peanut Buster Parfait is my favorite indulgence. I don't indulge before lunch, just as I didn't indulge my Pall Mall addiction before lunch when I was a smoker. But sometimes I do have the parfait before dinner. I could rationalize this by noting that I'll eat less for dinner and that the DQ is less caloric and less expensive than another choice, a Graeters's hot fudge sundae. Or I could say that I walked the mile-plus to the DQ and the mile-plus back home thus getting my exercise along with my chocolate-fix. But I have no desire to justify my self-serving. Nor any desire to join a twelve-step DQ recovery program.

My vintage Dairy Queen has been situated for the past fifty-years in front of a mini-strip mall. Two of the stores are vacant, now, and I fear the corner will be sold and the DQ closed. It is prime real estate.

The Dairy Queen is *so* not Historical Weybridge. Its gutters are underlit by fluorescent lights. The front windows are opaque, covered in primary-colored ads for its offerings. A neon-lit gigantuous soft-serve vanilla cone is suspended over the patio. Trash cans with helmets, looking like sentries, mark the patios corners. Stationed in the back are four dark green dumpsters. Full.

I am a regular along with other regulars. Coaches bring their kid teams. Winners and losers lap their soft-serves side-by-side. Divorced fathers bring their kids on Sunday visitation days. Grandparents indulge their grandkids. Heavy-set women pop-in and pop-out, taking their indulgences to their SUV's, slurping Blizzards in private. High school kids used to walk over for lunch but now they are not allowed to leave the school at noon. The new superintendent thinks it is too dangerous.

"Peanut Buster Parfait," I say to Barbie, a tiny high-school aged girl behind the counter. "Lots of hot-fudge, please. And, I am a senior citizen."

Over the years, I have known some of the servers. Josh's girlfriend was one. At age sixteen, she achieved Assistant Manager. That status made her responsible for closing the store—making certain everything was clean, the sauces cooled, the money accounted for. Josh was at the DQ every night at closing time. One day, tired of sweet smells, his girlfriend quit in the middle of her shift, and Josh never went back.

"Two dollars and seventy-nine cents," Barbie says, giving me the senior discount.

I give her three dollars, and drop the change in the "Help the Children" jar.

Barbie pumps hot fudge into the bottom of the plastic glass, sprinkles on peanuts, a pump of vanilla soft-serve, more hot fudge and another pump of soft-serve, still more hot fudge and a spoonful of peanuts.

"Great," I say, picking up the parfait, a napkin and a red plastic long-handled spoon.

It's a warm enough early October afternoon to slip into one of the quarter-round cement benches on the patio and watch the activity around me. There are lots of different kinds of people coming. I have never seen the DQ so busy in the early afternoon on a school day. I'm having a great time. Peanut Buster Parfait and people-watching. What more could I want?

Perfectly satisfied, I walk back home.

Ernest is in the kitchen preparing yams and pork roast for our dinner.

"You won't believe what I saw at the Dairy Queen," I say, sitting down at the table and starting the conversation with an attention grabber.

"What?" He quickly puts the roast into the oven.

"There were all kinds of people there like I've never seen there before."

"What kind? Skinny kind?"

"No. Some kids with jeans hanging down past their underwear."

"Boxers?"

"I doubt it. They didn't look strong enough."

"Dogs?"

"Actually, there was an apricot-colored toy poodle there with a rhinestone leash attached to a svelte woman in high heels and a mini-skirt."

"So, her underwear was showing, too?"

"Not until she got into the passenger seat of a BMW."

"Anyone else of interest," Ernest turns his attention to olive oiling the yams.

"Yes. There were two youths speaking Spanish."

"Olé."

"And a carload of Upper Arlington types in their Abercrombie and Fitch T-shirts."

"Ubercrumby and Rich."

"And a woman pushing a stroller with no baby. And a guy who looked like Homer Simpson, although not yellow. And a trio of guys in Gahanna football jackets. A pit bull puppy on a string connected to woman with an LPN badge, and…"

"What were they eating?" Ernest asks.

I think a moment.

"I didn't notice," I say.

* * *

Over the next couple of weeks I go often to my Dairy Queen where this rapid shift in clientele has been taking place—different ethnicities, ages, races, social classes. Not only is the Dairy Queen's architecture so not Old Weybridge, now the clientele are so not old Weybridge either. I ponder the possible changes—a Weybridge "melting pot" to go with the DQ chocolate melter? An urbanized village? Sight-seers?

* * *

"You might want to read this," Ernest says. He hands me the Weybridge *ThisWeek* newspaper.

I read the headline: POLICE ARREST 13 YOUTH FOR TRAFFICKING IN HEROIN. And then the lead paragraphs: Weybridge police arrested thirteen young adults in a drug sweep at—

"—the Dairy Queen!" I cry.

"Yep," Ernest says. "*Your* Dairy Queen."

"OMG!"

"Yep."

I read on. "They were selling Mexican brown heroin."

"It's needle grade," Ernest says.

"Inexpensive," it says here. "Highly toxic. Highly addictive."

"Yep."

"They've been dealing at the DQ for three weeks."

"Yep."

I'm shaking. I hand the paper back to Ernest. "Read what the police sergeant says!"

Ernest reads out loud. "'In the past we dealt with weed, pills and some cocaine...All of the sudden, you're talking about heroin... Some kid will ruin his life.'"

I take back the paper and scan for names and addresses. Only one dealer lives in Weybridge.

"I feel for his parents," I say. "All the parents."

* * *

Two days later I go the Dairy Queen, glad that it is still open. Only the regular-regulars are there. I'm thinking about what the police sergeant had said—"Some kid could have ruined his life." I'm relieved it wasn't my kid. Twenty years ago it could have been. Would have been? But it wasn't.

SOLSTICE WRENS

Seven members of Women's Spirituality drift in, take seats on the worn couches and chairs surrounding the coffee table in Emerson Lounge. We are alone in the Church's stillness. Marilyn, the Church's treasurer, has the key. An unlit concrete sign marks the driveway: ALL ARE WELCOME. It is dark and cold outside.

Unlit white candles surround our Yule log, a tightly rolled newspaper, bound with duct tape. Gloria takes an array of books celebrating the Winter Solstice out of her knapsack and sets them on the table. "We're welcoming back the sun," she says. She reads to us about a solstice ritual in Ireland: "In days of yore, a mob of boys would go hunting for the first wren of winter, chanting,

'The wren, the wren, the king of all birds
Although he is little, his honor is great.'"

The "Wrenboys" would chase the "King Wren" over hills and dales, through privet and thicket, until it would fall, exhausted, to the ground. The nearest boy would smack it with a stick. Other Wrenboys would then pole-stab the King Wren and parade it about town, knocking on the doors of the rich, demanding a tuppence or two in exchange for a Wren's feather, a Celtic symbol of vibrancy, giving one a happy heart and reminding one to be kind to others.

"Well, I think we've heard enough about the Wrenboys," Gloria says, responding to the group's moans and shudders.

"Sorry, I'm so late," L'Toya says, coming in. She is our eighth member. "I just got off work."

We nod our welcomes.

"Anyone? I need to talk to someone!" A woman's loud voice coming down the hallway penetrates our room. "I dunno wha' to do." The voice grows louder.

Our once-upon-a-time-dancer, Emily, sitting closest to the door, sashays into the hallway. "The ministers aren't here," she says. Her voice is as sweet as a bluebird's call. "Can I help you?"

"I need to talk to someone. I dunno wha' to do."

"We're having a meeting," Emily says, "but come in."

The loud voice is attached to a large woman walking with a cane. "I dunno know wha' to do." She's crying. "My gramma was jes killed by that drunk driver up near Morrow—you know about that doncha?—and I don't got no money for gas."

"Take my seat," Emily says, re-settling her thin-self between Marilyn and me on the large couch.

The woman looks to be in her mid-thirties with that "such a pretty face" associated with the morbidly obese. Layers of fat cascade over her swollen abdomen onto her thighs as she settles in the comfy chair, resting her cane on its arm. "I'm sorry," she says, crying and sniffling. "Don't anyone got a Kleenex?"

Emily hands me a red and green Christmas Kleenex she had tucked in her belt. I hand it to the woman.

"Hmm… It smells good," she says. Her sobbing has abruptly stopped.

"What's your name," I ask. "Mine's Laurel."

"My gramma was killed by that drunk driver up in Morrow," she says, sobbing renewed, "and my 'lectricity is off and my mother's in Doctor's Hospital with breast cancer and I'm s'posed to bring her home…She lives with me…and I don't got no money for gas…And my children are hungry…They want milk and eggs…I have three boys…Two years apart."

The group looks as uneasy as I feel.

"I dunno wha' to do…Wha' to tell 'em…They're hungry for them milk and eggs…and they're all sick… well, two are sick…the youngest with leukemia and the next one with M.S…the oldest one, he's not sick… And my husband has left me 'cause the kids waz sick and I get no support money 'til Friday…I don't know wha' to do…"

Her litany stops. She seems to be waiting. Ella has put her head down, averting eye contact. Sarah, Roxie and Ruth avoid eye contact, too. Gloria looks disturbed.

The stranger's hair and hands are clean, clothes pressed, shoes unscuffed. She sits with her legs spread wide apart, her coat scraping the floor.

"Have you called the Red Cross?" Marilyn asks.

"They won't help no more in Columbus. Anymore they're with other people."

"Where do you live?" I ask, trying to think if there are any low-cost apartments nearby. I had wanted the Church to sponsor affordable housing on their High Street property but they sold it to a strip mall developer.

"Near the Quizmo," she answers. She points behind her with her thumb.

"There's a free taxi service for the hospital," Marilyn offers.

"My mother just had two hip replacements and she caint get in and out of the taxi."

"There's a hospital van," Marilyn counters.

"There use to be. I'm sorry to say this," the woman says looking at L'Toya, "but black men abused the van. They took money and abused the van and now it isn't there no more 'cause of them blacks."

L'Toya is impassive. We are all silent.

"There's *First Call*," Marilyn continues.

"You got a Children's Hospital sweatshirt on," the woman says to Marilyn. "Do you work there?"

Marilyn nods.

"Maybe you seen me. I'm there all the time with my youngest. He's got leukemia."

Marilyn shakes her head "no," and asks, "Who's watching the boys now?"

I admire Marilyn's social-worker skills. She's finding out the essentials without sounding accusative or invasive.

"My half-sister. She lives with us."

I admire the woman's ensnaring skills, too. She's drawing us in.

"My parents bin married fifty years," she says with pride. "When they were married for 25 years, my father had a midlife crisis." She looks knowingly at us, as if we all know about and believe the cultural story about men in mid-life. "The mother died and my mother said it wasn't the baby's fault and she took the baby in."

"*First Call* has services you can use," Marilyn reiterates.

"They don't never give out food. I called. They don't. I called. There's some church out East that does but I dunno where it is."

"How'd you happen to find our church?" I ask.

"My Aunt Marybelle told me about you. She comes here." The stranger pauses, looking at us face by face. "She's friends with your kitchen worker, Sue Ellen."

"You got the wrong church," Gloria says. "We don't have kitchen workers."

"What's your name?" I ask again.

"Missy," she says, half-smiling, looking proud, as if she has just made the name up especially for our group. "It's Missy."

Gloria's packing up the candles and Yule Log.

"The social worker at Doctor's Hospital can help you, Missy," Marilyn says.

"No one's there to help...I dunno wha' I'm goin' to do. My kids are hungry for milk and eggs."

"How'd you get here, Missy?" I ask.

"Huh?"

"Car? Bus? Foot?"

"My half-sister's Tracker," says Missy.

TRACKER! The gas guzzling behemoth that nearly ran Ernest and me down in the National Forest in Sedona. Gloria puts the Yule log, books and unlit candles into her knapsack.

"I'll be closing the Church soon," says Marilyn, handing a ten to Emily, who hands it to me. I take a twenty out of my wallet, wishing I had more. I hand the thirty dollars to Missy.

"Thank-you," Missy says, getting up. Holding her cane, she lumbers out of the lounge.

Women's Spirituality is now all talk:

"She's mentally disturbed."

"She's ignorant."

"She wanted our money not our help."

"How can you cook eggs without electricity?"

"Maybe she has gas."

"She probably didn't pay her electric bill."

"She's racist."

"She's definitely ignorant."

"I was robbed at the ATM by white men."

"I was robbed by white men, too."

"She knows the system."

"Not very well. She didn't know that *First Call* gives food."

"I mean the con-game system."

"The benefits in Ohio are really good. I came from Michigan so I could get them. There's ways of getting help. She doesn't have to do this."

"Maybe she'll use her money for alcohol."

"Or worse."

"She doesn't look that way to me."

"She didn't smell of smoke or alcohol."

"She's mentally disturbed."

Many of the group members nod their heads in assent.

Gloria hands each of us a lavender stuffed, small hand-sewn purple wren. "Princess Wrens," she says. " We hold hands and chant:

> The circle is open, but unbroken.
> Merry meet, merry greet and merry meet again!

* * *

There is no Missy, Missy half-sister or Tracker in the parking lot about which I am relieved. But with the new Church entrance visible from High Street, Missy is just the first, I think, of the "winter wrens." Can women be safe any longer at Church at night?

Driving home, my thoughts are not about safety, though, but about the claim we make at the Church: "All Are Welcome." Was Missy welcome? Are we prepared to embrace a kind of radical hospitality, where everyone is graciously received, acknowledged for their humanity, their divine spark? Or, is the "welcome" sign a hypocritical nicety? Code?

Do the Missies of the world disturb some of us enough to project onto them the label *"mentally disturbed?"* Do some of us think "mentally disturbed" is a less pernicious label than, say, con-woman? Liar? Poor?

Two of us gave Missy some money but none of us gave her emotional support. None of us invited her to take part in our solstice celebration. No one confronted her on her racist comments the way we would someone we considered our "equal" or "educable" or "sane." Why did we let her "agenda" dominate? Out of unspoken fears? Repressed angers? An unconscious sense that she was a "lesser" woman than we were? That she was not "like us"?

Pulling my Chrysler into my garage, I inhale deeply. Turning the car off, I shake involuntarily. I sit in the car's seat, shaking, as I realize that I might have been in a very dangerous situation and, worse, didn't know it, hadn't recognized the potential.

The last Tracker I had seen—in Sedona—had two vicious men in the cab with rifles in the gun rack. For all I know, "Tracker" is code for *predator*: Missy, a Wrenboy.

I come into the house, call to Ernest, tell him the story and go to sleep, giving thanks.

2003

DO NOT GO-LYTELY

Ernest parks our car in R Garage at the large teaching hospital. I have arrived for my colonoscopy appointment at 9:00 a.m. sharp. A nametagless man tells me my Medicare forms have not arrived. I must agree to pay for my "procedure" if insurance doesn't. He puts a paper I.D. bracelet with my name on it around my left wrist.

At 9:15, a nametagless woman calls my name.

"C'mon Ernest," I say.

"Sorry," Nametagless says. "New rules allow only the patient to come back. Privacy, you know. You can wait here." She points Ernest to a rectangle of thirty or so chairs, right off the elevators.

"If I get tired of reading," he says, "I can ride up and down the elevator."

"If you were a sociologist," I say, "you could research waiting behavior in this very public space in which to consider the privacy of a loved one."

"You'll be called after awhile," Nametagless says to Ernest. She ushers me through an automated door into the rectangular women's space, just long and wide enough to hold four armless chairs, side-by-side, along one wall. At the rear of the rectangle is a closet of a room, partially closed off where, I think, doctors can deliver bad news.

Sitting in the furthest chair is Trudy, a woman in her fifties. She's wearing a hospital issued washed out pink printed gown, covered with a washed out blue striped robe. She looks washed out, too. She's arrived an hour and a half late, but they are going to take her, anyway, she says.

"Who's your doctor," I ask Trudy.

"Williams."

"Williams is mine, too," I say. "He's very experienced. I phoned and verified that he would do the procedure himself. Not pass it off to a resident."

Trudy likes to talk. She's had breast cancer and has had polyps removed from her colon. Only six months have passed since her last colonoscopy.

"I cheated a little, and ate some cereal yesterday," she says. "Williams always yells at me for not having a clean bowel. But I can't do what he wants."

91

"It's hard, I know," I say. "But I have followed his instructions totally." For two days I did not eat, and I drank all the lemon-lime Go-Lytley. "Plus," I want to say, but restrain myself, "I've arrived on time."

* * *

At 9:30, Melba joins us. She likes to talk, too. She tells us she's 82, divorced, a mother of two sons, a retiring football coach and an unemployed lobbyist. Both "boys" live at home and "can't do a thing around the house."

"I've never been cut," Melba says in a Kentucky accent, as her hand criss-crosses her gut. "Dr. Brenner took a malignant polyp out of me twenty-five years ago. He jes took it right out of my rectum. No cuts."

"Hmm," I comment, opening up my *Prevention* magazine.

"Did you have radiation?" Trudy asks.

"Nope. Never had to."

Trudy looks dubious.

"Have you ever seen a polyp?" Melba asks.

"No," says Trudy.

"It's jes like a seed. Dr. Brenner lost one in me and he took it out and showed it to me and I said it looks jes like a strawberry seed. That li'l strawberry seed jes grows and grows."

I keep my mouth shut and eyes focused on *Prevention.*

Ella joins us at 10:00. She's from Mansfield. Her hair is dyed, permed, and coiffed. She's almost too wide for the last remaining chair. We are four sitting ducks in a row.

* * *

"You two can change now," Nametagless woman says sheparding Melba and me together into a smaller rectangular space with half-sized lockers.

"Lockers 7 and 8 are free. Change and choose one," she tells us." Leave the gown open down the back."

Melba's muttering about lucky numbers, but I'm changed first and go for Locker 7. I struggle to get the lock off its hook and the key off its safety pin. Melba calls for help.

"Will I go back soon?" I ask. I have hypoglycemia and am faint from lack of food and water.

"Not for a while," Nametagless woman says. "Trudy will go before you."

"Even though she was so late?"

"I don't make the decisions," Nametagless says. "I just work here."

"How long have you been waiting?" Ella asks, picking up my *Prevention* magazine, the only reading material in our space. She is shivering.

"Over an hour," I say.

At 10:30, I push the automated door button and half-shout, "Ernest."

He picks up his scuffed leather brief bag, the first present I ever gave him. When his classics professor brother-in-law saw it, he said, "Marry Her." I wave Ernest towards me. There are signs of great relief on his face.

"They've not even called me back, yet," I tell him. "I didn't want you to worry."

He does worry about me. He loves me…and needs me.

"Have you ever seen meaner eyes?" Ernest whispers to me, pointing to a prisoner on a gurney. Two men with badges and weapons flank the prisoner. A blanket has been crudely placed over his ankle chains. "Eyes with no soul…Raped."

The prisoner is wheeled back into the bowels of the men's pre-colonoscopy area. I return to the woman's rectangle. Trudy is called. Melba is called. A thin man is taken into the "bad-news" room to await his wife and her doctor. He smiles at the air, hopeful.

So much for privacy…

"Mrs. Richardson, there's a spot for you now," says Nametagless. I am on a cot that she wheels to a different, larger, waiting area. There are about a dozen of us on cots, men and women unshielded from each other's view. I see the prisoner.

Intersecting worlds.

"So, you're done," I say to Trudy who is in the cot next to mine.

"No. I haven't gone back yet," she answers.

It's 11:00. I fold my arms over my chest and try to sleep, try to blot out the cacophony, cross-talk, staff speech I don't want to hear:

"Mary! Why haven't you washed the scopes?"

"Do it yourself!"

"Dr. Brenner, your patient is ready for discharge." This on the loudspeaker.

"Dr. Friedman, you're wanted in consult." This, too, on the loudspeaker.

"You must have had a polypectomy." A man's sonorous voice.

"She doesn't speak English."

"The baby can't come back here."

"Mary, call for her son to come and translate."

"Call him yourself!"

"Quinn's goin' tear your hair out!"

"The hell with Quinn!"

"Who put *you* in charge?"

"Another prisoner in chains today?"

"Yeah! They always come on Monday!"

"I *have* to leave at noon!"

"Who's goin' wash the scopes?"

"What the hell! The camera didn't work! Why didn't the camera work!" I recognize Dr. Williams's voice. He sounds furious.

* * *

"Why are you having this procedure?" a disembodied, unidentified voice asks me.

I look at the back of a head. Its front is looking at my chart. No nametag.

"Because I have family history." I answer. "And my age."

"I *need* you now," someone yells at disembodied.

"Someone else will have to finish *her*, then," she retorts, as if she has won some battle. I am "her."

Trudy is wheeled away on her cot.

"Terrible veins...terrible," Nametagless II mutters, as she struggles to insert my I.V.

"What's wrong?" I ask.

"I'm not happy with its position."

"Will it affect my anesthesia?"

"Not likely," she says, "If it stays in."

I am fading away.

* * *

At 11:15, I am wheeled into Procedure Room 1 which is bright, cold, and uninhabited, except by me. Nametagless III comes in. She connects me to an electro-machine, measuring something or another, without looking at me or speaking. She peers into a computer screen.

"Are the uncleansed scopes they're talking about the colonoscopy scopes?" I ask.

"Yes," she answers. "That's all they do here, now. The doctors do the endoscopies at VillaFlora because they own it. They can do three or four endoscopies in the time it takes them to do one colonoscopy—and they get paid the same for either one of them. It's all about the money. They just want to keep making their money." She vents about her working conditions. I try to offer solutions—transfer, retire, organize. Her anger is palpable.

"You should write the Customer Relations Department," she tells me. "They won't listen to us."

"Why don't they have more scopes here?" I ask.

"Three of them are broken."

"Why don't they buy new ones?"

"They cost $28,000 each, that's why."

"That's just a couple hours of pay for an administrator here," I say.

Nametagless III doesn't laugh.

Nametagless IV comes in and attaches a scope to an instrument box.

"It's cleansed, right?" I ask. "I hope it's not the prisoner's scope."

She scoffs, shakes her head.

Nametagless V comes in, and says, "We're ready in Room 2, Mary." Mary disconnects my Room 1 scope and takes it away with her.

"Why do the scopes break?" I ask III.

"Computer chips go. Everything has a shelf life."

"Including your patients?" I ask.

"Some, yeah."

It's confusing for me not to know who is an aide, a nurse or a doctor. "Why doesn't anyone wear a nametag?" I ask.

"Don't ask me. I just work here."

At 11:30, Mary brings in a scope. "Quinn and Pat are going to kill each other," Mary says merrily.

"Quinn just snaps sometimes. I've seen him," says III. "Short fuse!" She clips something laser-like to my right index finger.

A Nametagless woman in a blue jacket comes in and signals for me to sign the *permission slip*, which I can't sign because my right index finger is freighted down.

"Take it off," she orders in an East Indian accent, pointing to the clip.

"I didn't know I could do so," I protest, taking it off, signing, and putting it back on.

I guess she started the anesthesia.

* * *

95

"Where am I?" I ask Nametagless II.

"In recovery," she says.

"What time is it?"

"Noon."

"Who did my scope?"

"Dr. Prem did but Dr. Williams was in the room all the time."

I feel had.

* * *

"Can you get up?" II asks. It is 1:15. There are three sets of three chairs across the room from the cots. I am sitting in one chair in one set, Trudy in another, and Melba in the third. We are triplets today. None of us is in the bad-news room today.

"Hi," Ernest says, coming in and sitting down next to me. It is 1:30.

"What's this?" he says, picking up the report sitting on the third chair.

"You can't have that," II says, trying to snatch the report out of Ernest's hand.

"I want to read it," Ernest says, holding on to it. "This is all good news," he says. "No polyps. No mention of diverticulosis. Do you realize how good this is?" No pathology, no cancer, I know he's saying "hurrah" to himself. The cancer history in my family is frightening.

Ernest replaces the chart on the third chair.

"Dr. Williams…your patient is ready for discharge," says a voice over the loudspeaker.

At 1:45, Dr. Williams picks up my chart, looks at it and mutters to himself—"Let's see who is *this*… oh, yes."He looks angrily at me. "You didn't follow my directions, did you?"

"She followed the directions assiduously," Ernest says. He likes defending me. "For two days to the letter."

"We did the best we could under the circumstances."

"So the results might not be accurate?" Ernest asks.

"Well, maybe the scope…" Dr. Williams stops himself. "I'll see her in 18 months."

"Twelve months," I say.

* * *

Ernest helps me walk back into the woman's waiting room.

"Is that the bad-news room?" Ernest asks Nametagless I.

"Good news, bad news, no news," she says, as if she had never seen the room before.

A heavy-set, well-dressed man is in there, reading my *Prevention* magazine.

"Do you have some pop? Crackers?" I ask Nametagless I.

"No. We don't keep that stuff," she says. "You can get your clothes on."

I go into the changing space, drop my robe into a receptacle, but I can't open the locker. I half-back out into the changing space and call Ernest for help.

He whispers, "What a beautiful ass."

THIRD ACTS

What a difference a few years have made. On our corner, the Vet Clinic is now the A-1 Relaxation Massage, and the Starbucks, having been torched by an ideologically motivated customer (someone we actually knew from Church), has been torn down and replaced with a locally owned bagel store. Further down High Street, a FOR SALE sign sits on a boarded-up window of Dawn's Dog Grooming and Boarding. The 150 year old brick building, once a school, looks anachronistic next to its neighboring shopping strip stores selling "Just Pies" and the oxymoronically named "Liberty Taxes." "Taco Parisio" is now a crematorium and a "chicken finger" restaurant is "Coming Soon" as is the preposterously named "E-Z Car Wash."

Empty lots. Empty stores. All the way from Weybridge into Clintonville where I am going for a poetry reading by my friend and favorite local poet, Liz James. She last read at the Areopagetica Used Book Store, the poetry community's mainstay. But now the bookstore is closed, unable to compete with Amazon.com.

The poetry readings have moved a few blocks down High Street to Pearls of Wisdom, a New Age store that sells books, charms, stones, crystals, music, prints, and Power Pyramids. Thirty years ago, I bought two crystal and amethyst wands here to which I attached the two silver baby-shoe charms (one for Ben, one for Josh) that my mother had worn on a silver chain. I take the wands and charms with me when I fly. Just in case.

Pearls of Wisdom was once a graceful house sitting near other graceful houses in which successful Columbus families resided. But, High Street became a boisterous street, the main north/south thoroughfare in Columbus. Families no longer wanted to live there. Fortunately, the houses were rezoned as commercial property, a decision that has kept them from being razed and replaced by strips of strip malls.

Five stone steps with wrought iron banisters lead to Pearl of Wisdom's entry. Incense is burning. In the back of the store, there is a large room for spiritual gatherings, past-life regressions, astrology-training, animal-communication, and, now, poetry readings. About a dozen people sit in a semi-circle around the organizer, Dianne. A clutch of opened umbrellas are drying on the wide-plank floor.

"I'm sorry, I'm a little late," I say to Dianne. She is wrapped in a purple shawl, her signature color. "I had trouble finding parking." Now cars can only park on one side of High Street during the newly instituted extended rush hours. "The rain isn't helping any either."

"Glad you are here," Dianne says. Her voice sounds crackly; she moves gingerly.

"What happened to your arm?" I ask, noticing the sling beneath the shawl. "And your face?" She is badly bruised around her eyes.

"I fell. I am lucky it wasn't worse."

Dianne tells me her story of slipping on the wet-floor in the bathroom, trying to catch herself, dislocating her shoulder and hitting her head on the sink.

"I'm so sorry," I say. "Anything I can do to help?" I know better than to have asked that question, but it is too late.

"Can you drive me home after the reading? My son drove me here, but I hate to ask him to help me *again*. He's been doing so much for me..." Her voice trails off.

"I'll be glad to," I say. This is an opportunity for me to "pay it backwards," to repay a little to Dianne for all the good things she has done, not necessarily for me, but for the literary community in Columbus. For decades, she has organized readings in open spaces like this one and in closed ones like addiction treatment centers and prisons. "Be glad to," I repeat more loudly as Dianne's wincing has perhaps drowned out my words.

"Glad you are here," she says to all the late comers. In the background I hear their apologies for tardiness.

* * *

"I'd like to write poetry again," I had said to my friend Ellin Carter way back in 1971. We had come in and out of each other's lives for decades— theater at the University of Chicago, Math Wives Club at Ohio State University, professors at OSU, Cat Welfare, NOW, Church, Metropolitan Progressive Elementary School, and now divorced single mothers. We had literally bumped into each other one afternoon as we were leaving our campus buildings. I began ranting with an abandon I reserve for long-time friends. "I'm bored with writing like a sociologist." Having surprised myself for having said so, I realized that I was.

"Come to the women's poetry writing group," Ellin suggested. "It's an offshoot of a poetry class I taught last quarter. We're meeting weekly."

"But," I stammered, "I haven't written poetry for twenty years or more."

"It's a workshop! Come!" She brushed a strand of red hair off her cheek.

"But…"

"Every Tuesday at noon in the English Department's seminar room."

"But…"

"See you there…Oh, and you don't have to bring a poem the first time you come."

Kabalistic tradition says that some of the people that come in and out of your life at propitious moments are *your angels* here on earth. I think Ellin was one of my angels. She was a friend when I had experienced the car accident, coma, and subsequent aphasia. She encouraged me to write as a way to regain control of language. I followed her advice. My first post-accident paper reflected the jumbledness of my brain, my mixing up of my sociological interests with classical literature I had studied in college. "An Analysis of Power in *Paradise Lost*" was a weird paper, but a first-rate journal published it, giving me confidence that I could recover.

Perhaps, we were *angels for each other.* When her daughter, teen-aged and willful, ran away with a questionable man, Ellin asked Ernest and me to sit with her during the overnight vigil. We were there to welcome back home the wayward daughter who subsequently grew into a kind and loving woman. And, when Ellin's son was diagnosed with a learning problem, I led him to his college's disability services.

When I arrived at my first poetry workshop, ten women were sitting around a seminar table. Mimeo machines growled. Ellin's red hair framed the mischief in her eyes. "Let's introduce ourselves," she said. "Tell us what animal you are, and then, if you wish, your name."

"I'm a jaguar," I said. "And my name is *Laurel Richardson.*" *Whoops! What's gotten into me? Why didn't I use the name I have gone by for decades, my married name, my professional name, Laurel Walum? Why did I use my birth name?*

"Help yourselves," Ellin said, pointing to poetry magazines piled high around her, tapping an "excellent" one. She passed out flyers announcing poetry events and contests. "So who's brought poetry? "Remember," Ellin said, pointing to the small folded signboard in the middle of the table, "NO APOLOGIES!"

Ellin guided the workshop members into what she called "empathetic critique." Every poet was respected, listened to, helped with technical problems, voice, and insecurities. The following week, I brought my first poem. I didn't apologize out loud, but its title,"*Dream Scratching I,*" announced my insecurity and the possibility that I might write more poems.

"An absolutely remarkable first poem," Ellin said.

Ellin's mentoring changed how I wrote sociology. I found myself writing breath points, unconventional paragraph breaks (like line-breaks), alliteration, assonance, metaphors. My writing had to pass the "reading-aloud" test. And, I integrated what had been a divided writing-self into one name: *Laurel Richardson.*

When I found myself unable to write-up an interview with an unwed mother in the standard sociological way—snippets and commentary, looking for themes—because to do so felt like a violation of her actual experience and her trust in me, I turned the interview into a narrative poem, retaining the woman's words, rhythms, and voice. "*Louisa May: The Story of Her Life*" changed how sociological findings could and would be written over the next decades. It helped resuscitate humanistic social-science and welcomed in marginalized persons, and different ways of knowing and telling.

For the next thirty-years what became known as Women's Poetry Workshop (WPW) met on a regular basis and helped create a Columbus that welcomed not just poetry but feminist processes of inclusion and openness.

"That downtown storefront is empty," Kezia noted. "Perhaps we can convince the owner to let us use it for walk-in poetry readings. Open to everyone." And with that, TUESDAY NOONS: POETRY READING became a downtown Mecca for office workers, sales folks, and the homeless.

"I need poets to tell the story of my life as I dance it," Nancy Fenster said. And with that, WPW wrote poems for her and performed with her, enacting feminist collaboration across art-forms.

"We need to share our process and poems," Ellin said. And with that, over the years, WPW published three volumes, *Righting, Re-Righting,* and *Write Again!*, hiring women artists and photographers and leaving copies in women's spaces, like twelve-step recovery Amethyst House and The Free Clinic.

"You need to teach more people about poetry," we said to Ellin. And with that she penned a weekly column, "The Writing Workshop," for the *Columbus Dispatch.*

"We need a literary venue for poetry," Jennifer Bosveld said, and, with that founded *Pudding House*, which became the largest independent publisher of poetry in the nation.

"We need to engage more young people," Liz James said. And with that came poets as mentors in the schools.

"More has to happen citywide," said Cathy. "Poetry Central" poetry everywhere: poems on sign boards on busses; poetry rea at the Governor's Mansion; spin-off poetry groups, mentored by members; and poetry in the parks. During the summers hundreds o listeners sat on blankets around the gazebo at Whetstone Park to hear local and national poets. When Alan Ginsburg came, there was Standing-Room-Only.

When Ellin died, WPW died.

* * *

"Laurel." Dianne's voice brings me out of my reverie. "We're ready to start."

"Where's Liz?" I ask.

"She's too sick to come," Dianne says. "Didn't I tell you? She wants you to read these poems. Probably, I didn't. I'm distracted." Dianne hands me a sheaf of typed poetry, with cross-outs and inked-in changes in Liz's handwriting.

"What's wrong with Liz?" I ask. For as long as I have known Liz, she has worried about her health, sure she was going to die before her time.

"Heart problems," Dianne whispers.

I am able to sight read poetry honoring its breath-points and meanings and I have no performance anxiety. Actually, I like to perform. But, to read Liz's poems—magically convoluted, breathy, mythic, long—to this audience that came to *hear* Liz was beyond daunting.

I begin, "I know Liz will be happy to hear that you have all come out on this rainy night to hear her read," I look at the mostly gray-haired audience. "And, like you, I am saddened to learn she is too ill to be here herself. But she has sent some poems and asked me to read them. I am honored. But, if I misread, please accept that like the rule that WPW lived by I will offer no apologies.

I stumble through fifteen minutes of Liz's magical realism.

"Open mic" Dianne says. "Please limit yourselves to one poem only." Sixty more minutes pass. Everyone but Dianne and I have left.

"Ready to be driven home, Dianne?" I ask. I locate her raincoat, put her good arm into a sleeve, the hood over her head, and pull the rest of the coat over her sling. "There, Little Red-Riding Hood," I say, snapping the snaps. But Dianne is not amused. She is trying to catch her breath.

"Are you okay?" I ask.

more quickly and shallowly. "I have a congestive

I take Dianne's good arm and walk slowly,
ighs more than I do but I will myself to hold her
as we mince towards the door. "I'll get my car
you okay?"

I'll just wait inside." She coughs.

The rain pelts me as I get my car and bring it to a "NO STOPPING" yellow curb in front of Pearls of Wisdom.

"I'll support you as we go down the stairs," I say to Dianne. "Can you hold the banister with your good arm?…Easy does it…There's no hurry… We can take our time…Here's my car…I'll open the door and help you in… There…I'll close it…Here, I'll fix the seat-belt."

"Ouch!"

"We can drive without it…I'll go slowly."

Dianne lives less than a mile away on another busy street in another old graceful house surrounded by other graceful houses. But these have not been rezoned commercial. If they were houses in Chicago or San Francisco, they'd be selling for multi-millions. But here, they are modestly priced, many owned by university faculty, some sub-divided into apartments. I think before too many years go by they will be turned into condos, and not razed, if we are lucky. I pull into the ruins of her driveway, a mine-field of flooded potholes.

"Ring the bell," Dianne says. "Knock on the door. My son can help me from here."

I negotiate the mine-field and slosh through the puddles on the broken brick walkway. I grab onto a slick banister as I slip/slide up the wooden steps to the uncovered porch. The rain does not stop. I ring the bell. No answer. I ring again. No answer. I knock…I knock…I knock…

"Nobody seems to be home," I say to Dianne after I slosh my way back to the car.

"I have a key," she says.

"Let me help you out."

"Ouch…"

"I'm so sorry."

"Oh…ah…ouch."

"I'm sorry…so sorry."

We make it up the stairs onto the porch and Dianne opens the door with her key.

104

"Oh, it's *you*." I hear a growly man's voice. "Back already?"

"Thanks, Laurel," Dianne whispers. "My son will help me the rest of the way."

"G'night, Dianne."

Good night, Laurel! What was I thinking? I am uncomfortable driving at night in the best of weather and scared-out-of-my-wits when it is raining. What did I do? I drove a passenger in the "death seat" without a seat-belt. I don't know how to protect a dislocated shoulder and worse I don't have the slightest idea of how congestive heart failure might show itself. Why didn't I call 9-1-1? Why didn't I have her son pick her up? What kind of magical powers did I think I had? I guess I wanted so much to repay her in some little way for all the good she has done that my rational mind abandoned me. Did I think that I might never see her again?

Or was it all that magical realism in Liz's poems. Or, maybe, Angel Ellin stopped by. Well, okay, then. NO APOLOGIES.

TRANSITS
2004–2008

There's always something...

– Rose Richardson

LINCOLN PARK

My mother's biological father, Beril, was a ferrier in a stetl outside Kiev. He was a master blacksmith and a learned man. With the czarist threat unfolding, he and his brother came to America to start new lives. They came to the Jewish ghetto in Milwaukee and opened a candy store. Three years passed before Grampa had the money to send for his wife and their three children. My eight-year old mother was the eldest.

Gramma left the stetl with what she could carry on her back; the children held each other's hands, none of them daring to look back on their village in flames lest they be turned into pillars of salt.

They walked to Kiev, took a train to Norway, found passage in steerage on a Norwegian freight ship. Grampa Beril met them at Ellis Island and brought them by train to Milwaukee to his apartment above the candy store.

* * *

Six months passed.
Gramma's keening could be heard all over Milwaukee.
The children wept, hugged.
"Gott in Himmel! Gott in Himmel!" Jews cried out.
Grampa was dead.
In the street.
Kicked in the head.
By a horse.

* * *

I never met Grampa Beril. I was forty-years old, picnicking with my mother's sister in Chicago's Lincoln Park, when she told me the story. But I had been collecting horses and horse stories much of my life, not in the nine-year old girl way with the unrequitable love affair with the horse. Rather, I had a conflicted relationship: love and fear. I loved and feared their power. They could bite. They could kick. They could nuzzle and eat apples from your hand. They could kill.

* * *

Ernest and I go to St. Petersburg, Russia when we are in our sixties. Although I had never been there, I can almost understand the Russian, but not quite; the cadences and vowel stresses are familiar. I recognize a small baroque-style mansion and insist we go inside. "The wallpaper's been changed!" I say to Ernest. On a lark, when I am back home, I make an appointment to see a psychic, who says, "In your last life, you lived in St. Petersburg. You were a radical young woman born into a merchant family. You had decided to leave your home to help in the revolution. You ordered a horse-carriage. The horse kicked you. You died."

* * *

"Look, you were walking in the street," the police captain in Mackinac Island said. "That's horse territory."
   "The horse and carriage were blocking the sidewalk."
   "So file a complaint."
   The horse had bitten my left arm, below the shoulder.

* * *

Father was in the Cavalry and trained General John J. Pershing's horse. I have photos of father standing beside that horse, holding its reins as it rears. That horse hoofed Father and for the rest of his life Father had ankle pain and a barely perceptible limp.

* * *

"The horseshoe's prongs should face up so that any good luck that's passing by can be stored," Father said when I was a child. "The horseshoe's prongs should face down so the good luck it has captured can flow out, surround the home and protect you," Father said when I was an adult.

* * *

Twenty-years ago I gathered together some yard leavings, a corn-cob, a crow feather, moss, leaves, dog hair and made myself a gentle companion, a sweet mare.

* * *

When I was a young woman, I would let my hair grow into a ponytail so long that I could sit on it. With each major change in my life, I cut my mane. My last pony-tail, cut when I was pregnant with Josh, is in a box on a basement book shelf. It is fifteen-inches long. A strong rubber-band secures all the strands. My grand-daughters like looking at it, taking it out, and pretend pinning it to their heads. I have always intended to send it to "Lots of Locks," a charity that makes wigs for children after chemo, but I never seem to make it happen. There is always something else that needs to be done.

* * *

Yesterday, I created a logo of my entwined initials, LR, a fearless horse.

* * *

HORSES

On the carousel
Round and round
Father beside me
Whistling

Plaster of Paris
Released from her
Rubber mold
Neighing

Silver
On the Silver Screen
Nuzzling my dreams

In ocean foam
A hitch of
White Horses
Galloping home

MY LAST CLASS

"You've been a great class," I say to the students in my last seminar. These are the same words I have said for over thirty-five years to other students. I sit on the edge of the Formica and steel teacher's desk and look around the low-ceilinged basement classroom. My foot hurts. I kick off my shoe. Faint smells of ammonia, fries and chalk-dust intermingle. The asphalt-tile floor is stained and littered. The fluorescent lights flicker. Sitting in their Formica and steel chair-desks, thirty-three dissertation students cram together in semi-circles.

Among the students there is a clutch of Ohio raised Euro-Americans, Asian-Americans and African-Americans but most of the students have come from faraway places—Turkey, South Africa, India, China, Japan, South Korea, Formosa, Thailand, Nigeria, Canada and Boston. They have come to earn their Ph.D.'s at The Ohio State University's premier Cultural Studies program in the College of Education.

I have taken an "early retirement buyout" from my home department, Sociology, not only for the pension benefits but for my mental and physical health. The Sociology Department had bought into the University's new "corporate model" of education. More. Faster. Qualitative research and teaching were devalued. Grant money! Numbers! I lectured four-thousand Sociology 101 students and supervised ten teaching-assistants who led the 100 student discussion classes. Neither my body nor my soul could tolerate the climate change. I couldn't stand it. Figuratively and literally.

But the "R" word scared me. I associated *retirement*—the word, the status—with being old, used-up, non-productive, invisible. And those were the positive associations. A more profound and scary association was that retirement meant *death* would soon follow. This had been the fate of my father and many *men* in the generations before mine. "Here's your watch. Thank you for your service." Three years later the watches stop ticking. My "watch" was a faux-metal medal in a genuine cardboard box.

But I am not a man, I tell myself. This is not the twentieth-century. I am not sick, only dealing with foot-pain. I have energy and knowledge. It would be morally remiss and emotionally distressful to stop teaching.

The Chair of Cultural Studies offers me a position as a Distinguished Adjunct Professor. He gives me the loveliest university office I had ever had—high up, modern, private.

For three years, I taught two writing seminars, each topped with fifteen doctoral students. I found the teaching load challenging, but doable because time was built-in for individual consultations. For three years, I had the premier academic job of teaching and learning. And no committees and no academic politics.

But this year the Chair has left and a new program director has been hired. He collapsed my two seminars into one, halving the students' access time and halving my salary. Corporatization of the university had reached the Cultural Studies Program. Retirement decision time. Again.

Six months earlier, my orthopedist had diagnosed my severe foot pain as plantar fasciitis, requiring thrice weekly physical therapy. Walking, driving, and sleeping (wrong) were excruciating. No shoes or inserts helped. I was issued a disability parking pass. Sometimes, I lucked out and found a parking spot.

I emailed the new director telling him that due to my foot problem, I would not be able to teach winter quarter. He emailed back from Tahiti where he was vacationing that, because I had signed a contract, he was prepared to sue me if I didn't teach. I was naïve. I didn't know that someone cannot be sued if they are physically unable to fulfill a contract. So here I am. Teaching.

But his bureaucratic and legalistic response to my pain cued me that it was not just my foot that was in pain: so was the rest of me. Emotionally and psychologically, I was through. I was finished investing my time and energy in *any* academic position.

* * *

Ten minutes are still left in the seminar. I fill them with my favorite question, "Any questions?"

"Will you serve on my dissertation?" asks the woman from South Africa.

"Mine?" asks the Canadian.

"Mine?" asks a Columbusite.

"No," I say "I am an adjunct. The University has to commit to you. It has to hire more tenure-track faculty."Four Cultural Studies positions had been vacated and not filled.

"You're the first professor who has encouraged me to think for myself," says the Nigerian.

"This class has been a gift," says the Korean. "Thank you."

"Will you be teaching the writing course next quarter?" asks the Formosan.

"No. I'll be in Hawaii."

"When will you be teaching?" asks the Turkish man.

I shrug. I hedge. I don't tell them they are my last class. How can you tell students who are raring to go into the academic world that you are champing at the bit to get out? It's unseemly and rude. And, if I had started to talk about it, where would it have gone? Would I be adding to the *morale* decay?

"Hand in your final work, please, and I'll get the grades in fast," I tell the seminar. An avalanche of folders cover my desk. I stuff them into two extra-large totes and carry the mass down the football-field length of hallway, up a flight of marble stairs, past a broken water-fountain, down the crumbled cement stairs to my car thankfully parked nearby in the side-lot, in the sole disability parking spot.

My plan, given the large number of students and the excessive amount of writing each one has handed in, is to graze here and there in their texts, write a word here and there—"good" or "develop more"—and then give them all "A's."

* * *

When I get home, I take a nap. When I wake up, I realize my grazing grading plan is not going to work. I've never been a lazy teacher and I can't start now. But it is hard to stay focused on the students' papers. It is really hard because I am not only leaving the university, I making a break from the academic model that has organized my life: time, energy. *Dressing.*

I am leaving the space in which I have shown my worth, value, right to be alive—ah, indeed my virtues—largesse, creativity, intelligence, integrity. *Get off you show-pony, already Laurel!*

There is a whole world out there. So many fields in which to play.

"Finished grading?" Ernest asks, noting my far-away look.

I check my grade-book. "Damn! Three papers haven't been turned in! I hate that about teaching!" I am surprised at the intensity of my feelings. My emotions stampede like a herd of wild horses. Grief, Sorrow, Happiness, Anticipation, Surprise, Anger, Inanition, Fullness, Wonder, Fear …

"Yeah," Ernest the Emeritus Professor says and quotes a line from *Godfather II.* "'Jus when you think you're finished…'"

CUT LOOSE

Monday night, after thirty-five years as a professor, I teach my last university class. Tuesday night, I turn in my grades. Wednesday morning, I go shopping at Nordstrom's. Everything looks awful, and even more awful on me. I see fleshiness, fatness, crinkles in the three-way mirror.

My face. *Aargh*! Colors clash with my skin tones. The styles accent my disappearing chin. Eyebrow a frayed scar over my right eye. Sagging mouth. Jowls. Furrows twixt nose and lips. A worn-out mare.

* * *

"Don't put yourself through this," Ernest says."You're beautiful. No woman is more beautiful than you. Wear what you have."

"My bathing suits are twelve years old!" I say.

"So what?" Ernest says.

"The hems are frayed," I say.

"Who cares?" Ernest says.

"All of Hawaii?"

Hawaii is where we will be a month from now.

* * *

At Otani's Japanese Restaurant that same night, drinking Kirin, I tell Ernest, "I *absolutely* cannot stand how I look!"

"Listen, Laurel…," Ernest is mumbling through a mouthful of raw Yellow Tail Tuna. "I love how you look."

"You must be in love with my brain."

"That, too. Def…nitely."

Last month, my ophthalmologist, concerned that one of my eyes was protruding, ordered CAT scans of my entire brain and eye orbits. The non-invasive scan required no prep and took only minutes. The next day, I received a phone call from the radiologist.

"Dr. Richardson?" he said. "This Dr. Diebald."

"Yes?" My anxiety is rising.

"I wanted you to know that you have no lesions, shrinkage, holes, atrophy. All hemispheres are fine—alive and active."

"That's good!"

"There's more," he says.

"Uh-oh."

"You have a *perfect* brain."

"Is that bad?"

"Hardly." The radiologist chuckles. "I've never seen one before. In an adult. Drugs…Alcohol…contusions…I called the staff in. 'Look,' I said, 'You'll never see the likes of this again.'"

"After all my brain has been through," I say to Ernest between bites of veggie sushi.

"What a perfect rejoinder for anyone who thinks you're retiring because your mind is shot."

I flip a piece of ginger at him. "I'm having cosmetic surgery," I announce. "So I can have a face that matches my brain."

"Ha-ha," he says and stuffs his mouth with rice and raw fish.

"I mean it."

He masticates and swallows. "You're actually serious?"

"I even hate how my hair looks," I say as the "designated driver" drives us home from Otani's.

"Now that," Ernest says, petting my hair, "is easily fixed."

Ernest is pulling implements from an upstairs bathroom drawer. "Your hairdressers haven't done it right for years," he says.

For decades, Ernest has wanted to cut my hair. He cuts his own baby-fine tresses and simply snips off his little ringlets. My hair is thick, coarse and straight.

"My hair is not like yours," I tell him.

"Not a problem."Mister Ernest wields his electric clipper. "Ready…set…"

"Okay." *How can it possibly look any worse?* Definitely tipsy. I step out of my Dansco clogs so Ernest and I will be the same height. Employing successively smaller clipper blades, he chops his way through my mop. Dark hair rains down my T-shirt, down my back, between my toes. Brown hairy hills dot the white throw rug. My feet itch.

"Aren't you done?" I ask.

"It's not even," he says, attacking my bangs.

They litter the sink.

"I need to make the back a little shorter," he says, snipping at my nape.

"Now, are we done?"

"There's a piece sticking out."

"Just because it's sticking out doesn't mean…"

"Laurel, I know what I'm doing."

"What's that black stuff?" I ask, looking in our three-sided mirror. My hairline is as high as my ear lobe.

"Five-o-clock shadow on the back of your neck."

"Do something!"

"Have faith, Laurel." He's wielding my Lady Gillette.

"Ouch," I scream.

"Aftershave," he says.

"I smell like a man."

"The smell fades fast," he says. "I'm preventing hair follicle infections."

I study myself in the three-way mirror. The front of me does look better without long hair pulling down my face. But my nape looks blotchy red in the hand-held mirror Ernest in holding so that I can fully appreciate his work. My hair is more or less on an even plane, but patches stick out like bristle cones, like the pin-brush I use on our cats. Little cut-in waves splash across the back of my head. Brillo. My hair is a minefield of mixed metaphors.

"The back needs some feathering and layering," Mister Ernest says, picking up the scissors.

"Not now!" I shout. "No!"

"Okay." He puts the scissors down.

When I was four, I tucked my hair into a cap and put on long pants, cleverly disguising myself as a boy for the Purim party. The organizer, refusing to believe I was a girl, removed me from the costume parade. I sat alone in the auditorium fearing that I had actually somehow turned into a boy. Preschool children think their sex can change, the way their age, weight, and height do. Preschool traumas linger. As a tall adult with a non-curvy figure, I am distressed when I am mistaken for a man as has happened when a Kroger bag-boy called me "Sir." I'm a woman, damn it! Even if I have short hair.

"I look like a boy!" I exclaim.

"No, not at all like a boy," Ernest says.

"I can't believe I let you cut my hair."

After a brief pause, he says, "I'll show you something. Wait here."

I hear him moving swiftly downstairs. Returning, he says, "Here's the Family Camp photo from your desk."

The cluttered, chaotic landscape of my desk, where familiarity breeds invisibility. "So?" I say, taking the small crudely framed photo from his outstretched hand.

"Study it," he says. "Take your time."

I scan the ancient yellow print as though only now, at long last it is reaching the final stage of development, and I see the most beautiful seven-year old girl, glowing, happy, bursting with energy and life. Her haircut…

"Oh, Ernest! You've given me back my…my—"

"See what you get for letting someone who loves you cut your hair."

HEAVY METAL

"Can you help?" I ask MicroCenter's Associate Bill. His name-tag is pinned on the left-side pocket of a light blue shirt. My sister-in-law, who teaches etiquette classes, says the "left side is the right side" for name tags because it can be seen while shaking hands, a patriarchal ritual that proves you're not holding a weapon.

Associate Bill's hand is pushing a cart of computer ware onto the sidewalk in front of MicroCenter. My Chrysler 300m is in the fire lane. He doesn't attack it.

"As soon as I finish here," Associate Bill answers me. I watch him transfer computer ware from the cart to a white-haired man's gray SUV. He's bent over as if he has spent his life at a keyboard. I pull my shoulders back and suck in my gut.

"Can you take my Dell to the repair desk?" I ask Bill. "I'll leave my car here. Okay?"

"No prob," Bill says.

My Dell computer is a wheezing seven-year-old and this past year has shown signs of electronic apnea. "It's going to crash, soon," my son Ben the computer-guy said. "You've got lots of time," my son Josh the other computer-guy said.

"I keep getting a warning signal that I have a Trojan—a horse? A condom?" I said to Ernest. "It tells me to download something to protect myself."

"Virtual condom for a virtual horse?" Ernest says.

"But no matter what I do the program will neither download nor go away. It keeps popping up, like—Oh, never mind." I stomped out of the kitchen into my study.

I called Josh again. "It's nothing," he said. "Ignore it."

I called Ben again. "It's serious," he said. "What's your security system?"

"MacAfee," I said."

"No wonder," he said. I can see him raising his eyebrows in disbelief that *his* mother has MacAfee. "Turn it off and bring it to MicroCenter."

"This is my Dell," I say to Associate Ashley at Repairs and Service. I try to sound proud.

Ashley flips her pony tail. She pats the Dell on its back as if burping it. She explains that it will cost $200 to check out the computer, reconfigure it, saving whatever files they can—but they are not promising anything about saving the files. They do promise, though, that all of my licensed programs will be obliterated.

"Even Windows?" I ask, incredulous.

Ashley nods.

"I'm not sure I even have the discs," I say. My voice is hoarse.

Ashley nods again.

"What will a new computer cost?" I ask.

"About $400," she says. "And you'll have Windows 7 op, 500 GB hard drive, dual core processor, 2 GB ram, and …"

But, I'm not really sure what she said.

"Ernest," I call his cellular phone from my cellular phone.

"Get a new one," he says, without hesitation. "But get them to take out your hard-drive and give it to you. Oh, and while you're there get me two 4 gigabyte flash drives."

"Take out the hard drive, please," I say to Ashley. She does. I leave my soft Dell in her capable hands, put the hard-drive in my back-pack and enter the bowels of the new MicroCenter.

In 1979, when MicroCenter opened its doors in a 900 square-foot storefront, I shook my head in wonderment: How could a whole store be devoted to computers? It'll be defunct, I thought, within the year. About computers I am always wrong. That little store invented the "technical department store," generated twenty-one other stores, a billion dollar a year business and its own brand of computer stuff. A few years ago they moved the landmark store into these 44,000 square feet of retail space, formerly a health-food superstore.

Like a supermarket, each of MicroCenter's twenty-two aisles have titles— surge protectors, AN cables, peripheral cables, printer ink, office supplies, media storage, games and toys, handsets, security, tools, keyboards, mice, cameras, networking-routers, networking-cards, speakers, notebook cases, mobile, cleaning. Even, software.

And HOT OFFERS.

Silvery bins between the aisles overflow with older software programs, tools, opened packages of cables and stuff that I have no idea what is. At the front of the store are six check-out stations plus "Repair and Service," "Returns and Exchanges" and "Pick-up Express" desks. A sign guarantees only eighteen minutes wait, if you've texted in your order. Whatever that is.

Around the walls, piled high with boxes, are The Departments—Technical Support, Peripherals, Portable Devices, Name Brand Systems (including their own brand, PowerSpec), Apple (I guess Mac's not a name brand), Books, and Gaming Department where a sixty-inch LCD is showing two cartoonish men boxing. Each of these departments is behind a wood-paneled wall and an arched doorway, as if to suggest you will enter a special room in the High-Tech Castle. As I bump into metal bins, I shake my head. *My God, they've outgrown this space, too!*

I make my way through the makeshift roundabouts in the aisles to the Named Brand Systems Department. Several customers are waiting for a sales associate. Everyone in MicroCenter is male, except for Ashley and me, and all the computers are sleek, silver and black, very yuppie masculine looking. The customers are looking at, reading about, and touching the equipment.

"I think I'm next," I say to the Manager Alex. He has just steered Associate Mike to a young guy who came in after I did. I feel like an invisible interloper.

"Mike just has to get a UBS cable," Manager Alex says. "Then Mike'll be with you."

"Of course, men are served first," I say to the young guy customer.

He smiles.

"I'm not surprised or angry," I say.

He's still smiling.

"I expect it." I deploy my credentials."I'm a Professor of Sociology at OSU who taught sociology of gender." I don't say I am retired.

"That was my favorite course," he says. His smile looks genuine now. "Inequality by race, class, and gender. I use it in my law practice."

"How can I help you," Associate Mike asks me.

"I need a new computer."

"Are you a gamer?" Mike asks.

"Probably not," I answer. *Whatever that is.*

"Download music?"

"No." *I don't know how.*

"Watch videos on your desktop?"

"Never!"

"What *do* you do?"

"Email, write…download photos."

"Got anyone to set up your system?" Mike asks.

"I have two computer experts. My sons. But they're busy and I don't like taking advantage of them."

"Mothers are the worst," Mike says.

"Worst?" I say.

"Actually, its grandmothers who are really the worst," he says.

"I'm both of those," I say.

"Well, then," Mike says, "you have two choices—Dell or PowerSpec. They're both easy to set up and the price and components are pretty much the same." He points to two silvery computers. Tweedledee and Tweedledum. "Excuse me a moment," he says. "While I help Mr. Armstrong at the sales desk."

I call Josh on my cell phone. "Which computer should I get?" I ask.

"An upgraded PowerSpec," he says, "because MicroCenter can repair it right there or give you a new one. Get 4 MB of ram though. And a quad core."

I call Ben.

"Get an upgraded PowerSpec," he says, "because MicroCenter can repair it right there or give you a new one. Get 4 MB of ram, though. And a quad core."

"I'll take an upgraded PowerSpec," I say to Mike when he returns, as if I am ordering a latte grande. He smells of cigarettes.

"Ready for a new LCD too?" Mike says, nodding at a shelf of monitors.

The twenty-one inch Dell sports a turquoise screen, a splash of ocean in this heavy metal land. "I like the Dell," I say, basking in its light.

"It's a very good monitor," Mike says. "It's the one I have."

"Do you say that to all the girls?"

"I think it's smart to upgrade everything at once," Mike says, soothingly, as he steers me toward the Peripherals Department. "That's what I do about every eighteen months or so. But I…"

I stop listening and start looking at the printers. They're all black and silver, too, like bad cowboys and AR15's. No women here, either—shopping or selling. Mike recommends an HP 6550. It looks like an aircraft carrier with levels and decks. It can print/scan like a Xerox, singles and multiples, fax and shoot down enemy missives. It takes a more expensive ink cartridge, but Mike assures me I'll get twice as much printing from it. MicroCenter is offering a no-interest one-year purchase plan on computers, plus, I'll get a $60.00 mail-in rebate from HP. Here's an offer I can't refuse.

Mike carts my choices to the Pick-Up Express desk, where Associate Chong hands me the paper work and asks for my driver's license. I start filling it in and start laughing.

"Why's funny?" he asks.

"*Physical* address," I say. "Like I would use my virtual address?"

"Why's funny?" he asks again.

"Jus' is," I say.

I complete the form and hand it back. Chong's eyes narrow.

"You wrote diffren' numbers on the side," he says, pointing to the right margin, "than you did in the blank."

"I couldn't quite remember my social security number. I use it so seldom."

He checks out my driver's license. *Do I not look like myself?*

"Your license expire," he says.

"Here's credit cards," I say.

"No. Mus' have picture."

"My Buckeye card?"

"No. Mus' be state issue."

"Passport, okay?" I say, searching for my Xerox copy.

"Mus' be original."

"Okay. I'll go home and get my passport. I live less than seven minutes away."

"Take your fill-in paper," Associate Chong says.

"All set?" Mike asks, reappearing at the just the right moment.

"Oh my God!" I blurt out to Mike. "I left my car in the fire lane."

"All the while you were here?" Mike asks, shaking his head. Was he thinking of his mother? Grandmother?

"I'm lucky I wasn't towed."

"Nah," Mike says. "We announce the car before towing. The last thing we want is an unhappy customer. We aim to please."

BLINDERS

I probably was near-sighted from an early age because I recognize people by their voices, gestures, movements, not by their faces. I never saw the sparrows in the elms or the little dipper or read the chalk writing on the blackboards until at twelve, I got my eyes tested—20–200, serious astigmatism, and a rare hyper-sensitivity to color.

My first pair of cat-eye glasses came in a jewelry box whose satiny interior secured a set of plastic inserts that I could weave into the frame so my glasses and clothing could always be color coordinated. Whatever I wore *had* to be color-matched. Had to be. I had glasses but I chose to wear them only when I *had* to see because I preferred my soft-edged fuzzy world to the hard-edged comic-strip world that my glasses created.

Because I had a heart-shaped face, my glasses *had* to be harlequin shaped. In college, black harlequins; in graduate school, tortoise; in teaching, back to multi-colored plastic inserts. Only when I turned thirty-five did I give in to wearing my glasses most of the time but still not when I was dressed up or getting my picture taken. My eyesight was 20–500—legally blind. Astigmatism, allergies and dry-eye syndrome collaborated; no matter how I tried, I could not wear contact lenses. Vanity be damned and gratitude be offered that glasses could correct my vision to legal driving eyesight, 20–40.

"Want to try again?" the bespectacled woman at the driver's license bureau asks. Because my license has expired, I need to take an eye exam to get a new one. I have twice failed to identify with my right eye when flashing lights appear on the screen.

"Let me try my left eye," I say. My hope is that I have peripheral vision in the left eye and that the testing-machine is programmed to repeat the same order of flashes for both eyes. So, if I can see the lights flash with my left eye and I can set my mind to remember their order, I can give those answers for my right eye, pass the driver's test, and get my license renewed. My plan works.

When I get home, I call Dr. Olsen at Capital Eyes for an appointment. "Your cataracts have ripened," he says, as if they were apples to be harvested. "Do you want to wear glasses?"

"Of course not," I say, thinking of how Ernest swoons over my unshielded brown eyes—"Deep" he says, "various depths, depending ...A window into your sweet soul—truthful, beautiful eyes"—and how I would feel young, again.

So, it was settled that I would have my clouded-over natural crystalline lenses removed and replaced by soft plastic apodized ReStor® lenses. They would provide me with long, mid-range and close vision. These lenses would cost me an extra $8000 but would be worth it. A good harvest for Dr. Olsen, plus I'd be saving the $800 a year my glasses now cost. In only ten years, I'd be even.

* * *

"My long distance sight is amazing," I tell Dr. Olsen. "I can see cracks in the Sedona rocks, hawks in flight, the little dipper, street signs."

"Color?" He asks.

"Fine. But I can't read."

"Be patient," he says at my first, second, third, fourth and fifth post-op visits. "I'm not abandoning you. The lenses are perfect. Give it time."

At the sixth post-op visit he refracts my astigmatism and suggests Plan A: an office operating room "little Lasik" procedure.

"What's Plan B?" I ask.

"You don't want to know," he says. "But I will tell you that your descended right brow causes your eyelid to droop, causing a lack of openness to the light and a deficiency in your near and peripheral vision."

Plan A fails. Despite the little Lasik procedure, I still can't read.

Time for Plan B.

* * *

"You're doing very well, Law-Rell."
"I bet you say that to all the girls."
"Only the pretty ones, Law-Rell."

I slip back into my Demerol-valium induced twilight sleep. I am lying on an operating table in the back room of The Aesthetics Center. I smell of betadine. Thirty-five years ago I was a passenger in a Volkswagen waiting at a red light behind a Mercury when a drunk driver rear-ended us, totaling the Volkswagen and the Mercury. I learned later that I had ricocheted twice through the windshield and that my cheek was broken, my jaw was broken, my right eye-socket was broken, and my right eye was lying in wetness on my cheek. I was in a coma.

An interning plastic surgeon repaired my face telling me that he had no choice but to repair my jaw off-center and sometime in the future the wax he had inserted in my cheek might migrate. He apologized for my droopy right eyebrow, but thought that it might repair itself once the nerves had regenerated.

For thirty-five years that right-eyebrow has continued to sag noticeably lower than the left one, narrowing the eyelid, diminishing the eye, requiring prisms in my eye-glass lenses, making me look sad, the crashed car trauma revisited every time I look in the mirror. For thirty-five years I have worn long bangs and thick designer frames that hide my brows. But now my ophthalmologist, Dr. Olsen, has told me that my descended right brow has seriously impaired my vision. So here I am.

"We'll do the brow first...Scalpel...Stapler."
"Ouch!"
"You're doing very well, Law Rell."

It feels as if screws are being driven into my skull. They are. Why am I here in this cold room on this hard bed with my cold hands clenching my stomach? I remember. Not only is it because of Dr. Olsen's "Plan B" to improve my vision—raise my eyebrow off the eyelid—it is because of Dr. Joan Carter's diagnoses. She is a naturopath whom I have been seeing for fifteen years. Because she has diagnosed and treated my digestive, energy and weight-gaining issues and because she has relieved my anxiety over imagined catastrophic diseases, I have great trust in her medical intuition— and the odd machine she hooks me up to test my body's "wisdom."

"You look tired," she had said, eyeing me while she handed me a metal bar to hold in my right hand, my feet on a rubber mat.

Biting my lip, looking down so she cannot see me too well, I heard myself talking to myself, *"You thought that by shedding your glasses you'd be magically back in your sweet fairy-land, young again, rather than old and haggard... indentations under your eyes sockets carved from sixty years of wearing glasses... eye bags deep enough to steep tea."* Out loud, I said "I know."

Joan eyed the computer screen that was "reading" my body. "You are more than skin-deep tired. Your drooping brow is affecting more than your sight. It's affecting your liver, kidneys, and Chi. And you are growing depressed."

I looked at her.

"I can offer some homeopathics," Joan continued, "but I think you should see Dr. Vinci. Insurance should pay for your brow problem." Joan studied my face. "He does mini-lifts, too. One of those would take years off you." She consults her machinery again. "Help your depression, too."

I looked at Joan's face and neck. She's sixty-two, recently divorced, and beautiful. I think she had a mini-lift herself. Joan hands me Dr. Vinci's card, and says, "He's a board-certified holistic plastic-surgeon. Holistic!"

Ouch!

Three weeks ago I met Dr. Vinci, a shortish-squarish-tannish man who wears golf shirts and khakis. He exudes the confidence and grace of a major league pitcher walking to the mound. His smile is wide as are his eyes. He is neither arrogant nor hesitant as he invites Ernest and me into his office, a quasi-modern functional affair, neither sparse nor exorbitant. An oil painting of an Etruscan woman is on the wall. I wonder if he knows that the Etruscans were the first people to train and breed horses. I wonder if he comes from Tuscany. I wonder why I keep wondering.

"What can I do for you Law Rell?" Dr. Vinci corrals my wandering mind. I like how he says my name, uplifting the second syllable.

I tell him about my car accident, migrating wax, nerve-damage, and impaired vision.

Ernest picks up a "before and after" photo book on the magazine table.

"Joan Carter sent me," I say.

"Ah! Joan," Dr. Vinci says, smiling even more widely. His eyes more merry.

"Are these photos of your work?" Ernest asks.

"Yes," Dr. Vinci shrugs. He picks up an ebony framed mirror, hands it to me and asks, "What do you like least about what you see?"

"My right eyebrow. My fat jowls. My fat neck. My marionette lines. My cheek scar. Eye bags. ..How sad I look...how tired—angry...old...so old." I blink back my tears.

Dr. Vinci looks over to Ernest and jokingly says, "I asked for one thing and she gives me this shopping list."

"I think she's beautiful just as she is," Ernest says. "It is not my idea for her be here. Whatever she wants and needs, though..."

"Keep holding the mirror Law Rell," Dr. Vinci says as he raises my brow with his fingers and lets it relax. Then he pulls my jowls under while slightly raising my cheek skin. He touches my off-center jaw. He touches my neck. "Your muscles are right out front," he says. "I can't do much to shape your neck. But I could give you a very very very small chin implant, Law Rell." He taps his own chin. "I have one." He takes a little piece of silicone from an ebony box on his desk. "I'd cut this way down. Very very very small. Re-center your chin. " He tweaks my skin back again.

I look in the mirror.

"This is what I can do," he says. Would you be happy with that Law Rell?"

I nod. I can't argue with Dr. Vinci. He is the expert. Charming, too. He hands me a Mini-Lift brochure. I put it in my purse. I will read it.

"Did you paint the picture of the Etruscan woman?" I ask.

"My brother did. He's the artist in the family," Dr. Vinci says, proudly.

"You're one, too," Ernest says, tapping the photo book.

* * *

"Scalpel."
"Ouch!"
"Forceps."
"Ouch, ouch, ouch!"
"You are doing very well, Law Rell."

I feel a tugging on my right cheek muscles, a wrenching, excruciating pain by my eye, and then I pass out again. I remember that I signed a patient consent form that said I might experience pain, but I thought it would be after the surgery, not during. *Why am I doing this?* How slow can a Mini-Lift be?

The brochure for the Mini-Lift appears in my mind, maybe in real time with the procedure. My father had a photographic memory. Maybe I do, too, when I am not-quite anesthetized. A steep bevel has been incised just inside my hair-line, meandering behind my ear-lobe and into the nape of my neck. The skin is elevated vertically and the underlying connective tissue is lifted and tightened...

"OUCH!!!!"

"Sorry, Law Rell. This always hurts."

...with a double-purse string technique, and the redundant skin is tailored.

Last month, I was listening to a symphony concert in the Chautauqua Amphitheater. I was by myself high up on the right side where I could see everyone in the audience. Most of the people were about my age. Everyone of them looked better than me—the bald man with the wart on his lip, the frizzy gray-haired woman with orange orangutan cheeks, the small chalky-white couple with matching patches of rosaceous, the myopic wrinkled-faced man, the tanned couple with outsize ears, the bloated sisters. Everyone had some noticeable disfigurement but none seemed as ugly as I did to myself: I was the ugliest person in the auditorium. I left before intermission so no one would have to see me.

When I had my car accident and coma, I lost my ability to do mathematics, think clearly, talk. But more than these, I had lost my sense of identity. Teaching statistics to university students was who I had been and who I no longer was. I transformed into a university professor who taught qualitative methods. When I retired, I lost that identity, too.

Now, another part of my identity has been lost. I am no longer a pretty woman. I am ugly. Age, accidents and sorrows have taken their toll. As I walk back to my rental, head lowered, I feel a deep sense of empathy for truly beautiful women, the supermodels. How terrible it must feel for them to age, to lose their looks, looks that are not shallow or just skin-deep, but in fact deep set elements of their identity. Face value is more than face value.

"Bo Ten."
"Cauterize here!"
"More Bo!"

Burning flesh. My flesh. I gag. It is not ugliness that has brought me here to this hard bed in a cold room. It is fear. When I look at myself without glasses, I no longer see *myself*. I see my older sister Jessica. I look like my sister. I look like her. I'm looking my *own* dying in the face.

"Law Rell?"
"Ahh?"
"Only the top-stitching left now...only seven-minutes left."

JESSICA

Twenty years ago, my sister Jessica's husband, diagnosed with congestive heart failure and rental failure, began sleeping on the living room couch; she began sleeping on the floor by the couch, like a dog. She monitored his water intake, his medications, his doctors' appointments and twice weekly IV infusions until her three late-stage unoperable cancers were diagnosed. Only after my sister spent six hours unable to get herself off the floor and out of her soiled mess, did John allow her to go to hospice.

I came at once. But John insisted that Jessica's "first rule" was "to get well," and her second rule was "to eat." He restricted her morphine. She was never out of pain, never allowed to tidy up her life. She died in unremitting pain in hospice in Des Moines.

John denied me the right to partake in her final minutes of life or to see her body after her spirit left. Within minutes of her death, John sent her to "science." No funeral, no memorial service, no candles lit in her memory.

A week after Jessica died, I adopted Asia, an undernourished, undersized, lap-kitten. She was nine-months old but had already given birth to a litter, all of whom had been adopted. Asia had not been adopted, the Cozy Cat adoption agent said, because she was black. People were superstitious.

Now it is a week later. This would have been Jessica's eightieth birthday. I gather my Ohio family—husband, children, grandchildren—together in my house for our own memorial service. In preparation, I purchased hand-made ceramic spheres, each unique in coloration, shape and heft, each with a hollow space in the middle.

The spheres are resting in my Gramma's copper serving dish in the middle of my round oak kitchen table. On a whim, I pick up Asia and set her on the table, too. She goes from family member to family member, mewing, asking to be picked up and loved. She goes to everyone.

"I think Jessica's spirit is inhabiting Asia," my granddaughter Shana says.

"I think so, too," I say.

We all nod. We each choose a sphere, take it to the flower garden, and slide it onto the upright copper rod pre-planted in the earth. Asia mews. Our totem glows in the late summer light. A yellow butterfly lands on the last

of the orange daylilies. Afterwards, we come in, sit around the round oak
kitchen table and have hot-fudge ice-cream sundaes.

REQUIEM

Rest, Jessica, rest.
No need to monitor
John's Temorin,
Salt, potassium,
Weight.
Rest, Jessica, rest.

No need to sleep
On the floor
Beside John on the couch

No need to get up
At four
Twice a week
For John's infusions.

No need to
Ignore your pain,
The mass in your colon
Your cancerous lungs.

Rest, Jessica, rest.
No need to feel
Needed.
Only my need
That you rest, Jessica, rest.

SECRET RECIPE

"Eleven dollars for a chicken!" I exclaim. Ernest has driven us to *our* Trader Joe's.

"They're on sale, Laurel," Ernest says. "Eleven bucks gets you two."

This is my first outing after my life-threatening allergic reaction to penicillin. My mouth and tongue were swollen, my throat was closing and it still feels clogged. *So this is how it feels to die an easy death,* I said to myself as I nodded off. Riverside ER saved me but I am hungry now and I must have chicken soup and Ernest hasn't been to the grocery in two weeks.

"You know, I don't much like chicken," he says

"I'm making chicken soup!" I loudly announce.

"Two for the price of one, Laurel." Ernest puts two chickens in the cart.

"Chicken soup is healing." I throw another chicken in the cart. "There!" I say.

Ernest puts in chicken number four.

Steroids and antibiotics have taken over my soul. I am in a rage one minute, weepy the next. "They're hormones, Mom," my son Josh, the molecular-geneticist, explained, to normalize my suffering.

I toss celery, carrot, onions, cheeses, cereal, rice milk into our cart, and a boatload of prepared frozen foods—Indian, Thai, Italian, French. Ernest limits himself to a frozen New York cream-cheese cake.

The narrow aisles of Trader Joe's are congested, festive. Customers come in mixed-race and same-sex couples. Chinese babies of Anglo mothers wave at Pakistani babies of head-covered mothers. A yamulked man guides his yamulked son to the kosher foods. An African-American woman and her Anglo partner discuss preservative free cereals with their twin girls, dressed in Mali cloth. Their children play hoppity-hop on the tile floor. A blond blue-eyed toddler joins them. A Downs' Syndrome child joins.

"We have the most open and integrated city in the world," I observe, "and suddenly they're all in my way...Not myself today am I?"

"Find everything you were looking for?" the red-faced check-out person, Caitlin, asks.

"I still can't find what I'm looking for," Ernest sing-answers with his Bono impersonation.

"What were you looking for?" Caitlin asks.

"He's kidding," I say.

"Oh. Ha-Ha," she says.

The computer screen says "$242.76."

"How insane!" I say to Ernest as he pushes our overburdened cart to our car. The parking lot is overburdened with gray-colored SUV's, CRV's, and Prius's.

"Food costs money," he says.

"Two weeks and inflation has skyrocketed! Insanity!"

"It's Trader Joe's, Laurel, and what we have is a cartful of bargains."

"Who can afford to make soup? The poor poor people," I whimper, collapsing onto the passenger seat.

"You don't need to help carrying in or putting away the groceries," Ernest says.

"Thanks. I wasn't planning to."

"Take a nap, "Ernest says.

That's what I've been doing for the past ten days. Napping. The trauma of near death, the harrowing experience of anaphalic shock, the replaying in my mind—I coulda died, didn't, but coulda. And the crazy emotional see-saw.

A week ago, the Columbus based "blended" family was at our house for family dinner, as they have been weekly for over a decade. There were ten of us at dinner—Josh and his family and Ernest's oldest daughter, Susan, and her family.

"Let's cancel," I had told Ernest. "I feel lousy."

"Not to worry," he said, "I've got this." He took two frozen lasagnas he had made a month ago and a scrunched bag of petite-peas from the freezer. "This will be just fine," he said, adding, "We have vanilla ice-cream for dessert."

"I almost died," I tell the families at the table. "This isn't my first brush with death, either …*Do you hear me? I almost died!!*…I almost died last week!"

"But she's okay now," Ernest said.

"No. I'm not," I said.

"Scary," Susan said. "Dying…" She looks at her father and blinks back tears. A few months ago, he had a "brain event." I rushed him to the ER at Riverside in the "car-car." He refused to give-up his little pocket-knife to the security guard. "Mine! Mine!" A triage nurse intervened and rushed him to an examination room. For two days, he was like a toddler asking the same question over and over again,"What time zit?" After peeing, he declared over and over again, "All better." He wasn't. He was in the hospital for five days. Susan spelled me part of the time. Doctors never figured out what had happened or why—nothing suspicious in his blood, heart, lungs, brain. "Idiopathic," was the diagnosis. *Idiotic pathetic doctors*, I'll say. But he is mostly recovered albeit more easily tired now.

"I almost died!" I scream. I can't stop thinking about *almost dying*. When I was six, I lay unconscious at the bottom of the Sovereign Pool. I had dived off the high board and not tipped-up my hands. When my head hit the pool's floor, I thought for just a moment that I had become a jelly-fish, soft and squishy. When I was eight, I lost my sense of *up* in a quarry. My breath ran out. A man, a stranger, pulled me up. When I was twelve and intent on swimming across Lake Geneva, a freak water spout separated me from the rowboat that accompanied me for safety. I floated on my back for what seemed an eternity, ready to give it up, when a patrol boat found me and officers pulled me from the water. When I was fourteen and being tested for my Red Cross Life-Savers badge, my instructor tried to drown me at the buoy, refusing to let me come up for air. My brother saved me.

"Do you hear me? I almost died!" I am shaking.

Josh gets up and hugs me. "You don't feel good, do you Mom?"

"No! I don't!"

"Well, what is everyone's favorite color?" Susan's little peacemaker Katie asks.

I insist that everyone answer her question: blue, green, black, black, yellow, green, blue, blue, blue, blue. *Now, congratulate me on joining our peacemaker in making peace!* No one does.

Then everyone is standing by the door, saying good-bye without having coddled me. I yell, "I bet you all wish I *had* died!"

* * *

Had my older siblings wished that? Wished that I had died?

"You were very sick when you were born," my older sister Jessica tells me. She is on her deathbed. She looks reluctant. "Mother was very sick with you. You were both in the hospital for over six weeks."

I am seventy years old. This is all news to me. I take her hand in mine. I can't tell where my skin stops and hers starts.

"I promised not to tell you," she says. Her eyes are dark, piercing.

"What? Not tell me what?"

137

"And we hated you," my brother Barrie yells, "because you took away our mother. We didn't want you."

Barrie leaves the room. Jessica zips her lips.

* * *

The natural, run-around free-range, no preservatives, no hormones cut-up chicken combined with organic carrots and celery, a few pinches of kosher salt, twists of pepper, a bouillon cube and filtered water is all I need to make chicken soup the way my Russian Jewish mother made it.

Mother started by washing off the chicken, placing it a large enamel pot, and covering it two inches past the wing tips with *cold* water. "*That's the secret.*" She added salt to release the "flavor in the bones" and for a "starter" a bouillon cube. "*That's the secret.*" She brought the soup to a simmer, skimmed it. "*That's the secret.*" She added cut-up carrots and celery and ground pepper, and brought it back to a simmer, where it bubbled for the next two or three hours. After it cooled, she separated the chicken and vegetables from the stock. "*That's the secret.*" She put everything in the refrigerator to "heal" for a day, "*that's the secret*," and for the chicken-fat to congeal, so it could be spooned away. "*That's the secret.*"

She never told me *the* "secret."

* * *

The smell of my chicken soup simmering on the stove pervades the kitchen, the basement, the dining room, my study. I am a child again. The scent is coming in through my nose and all the pores on my face and belly.

I phone my brother, Barrie, and tell him I'm making chicken soup the way our mother made it.

"So, am I invited?" He lives in Louisiana.

"My sense of smell is on steroids," I say.

"So, I should take a shower before I come?"

"Do steroids enhance all our senses?" I ask.

"Being alive sure does."

"The soup won't be ready until tomorrow. That gives you a day to clean up, suit up and show up!"

"Love 'ya, Honey," he says.

"Love you back."

"That soup does smell good," Ernest says. Its scent has tempted him up from his basement studio. He lifts the half-lid, hears the gurgles, reaches for a spoon.

"No tasting!" I say.

Mother never tasted her soup.

* * *

While the wide egg-noodles boil in salt water, I shred some white and dark chicken meat and toss it into the stock simmering on the stove re-stocked with the carrots and celery. *"Why would anyone toss out these good vegetables?"* I hear my mother's voice, see her shaking her head in bewilderment at the culinary extravagances of American Gentile women. In her housekeeping and child rearing practices she is an overachieving American housewife. The dishes aren't done until the broom is put away. Every day the bottom sheet on every bed becomes the top sheet and the top sheet goes into the laundry. Twice a week the Chinese hand-laundry picks it up and returns it in soft blue papers that are given to me because I like paper. Hand-embroidered name-of-the-day towels for each family member for each day, home-cooked hot lunch every day, children in their own rooms by seven o'clock when their father might be home and kiss them goodnight. Her French braided hair fixed, a clean dress and fresh nylons every evening. No one could ever again call her a *"dirty Jew."*

But in her cooking, she is her Russian Jewish mother's daughter. If she had not survived the pogroms, she would have been shot at Babi Yar and I would not be making chicken soup. I can't seem to remind myself of this often enough.

"Help yourself, Ernest," I say. I have put noodles in the bottom of each of our soup bowls and have ladled the chicken soup into mine.

"Any bones?" Ernest suspiciously asks, filling his bowl.

"Hope not. Eat carefully."

"My God, this is heaven," I say after my first swallow. "The flavor...the textures...the scent...the softness in my mouth...the taste."

"It is good," says Ernest adding hot sauce and soy.

"My taste buds are awakened." I rhapsodize. "Food has not tasted this good for years. And there are leftovers."

* * *

"Today, we'll have the chicken soup the way Gramma served it," I tell Ernest as I set the table. I had combined the noodles, broth and vegetables into one pot, heated it on the stove, and now ladle it into our bowls, sitting atop our dinner plates. Some leftover chicken pieces—a leg, thighs, a breast—I have served *cold* on a serving plate. As a side-dish, I have made baked apples with raisins and walnuts, ersatz tzimmes. Ernest pours himself a Diet Coke. I pour myself a glass of water. Ernest takes the breast and puts it in the micro-oven. I take a leg and put it on my plate.

"Hmm," I am ecstatic as a bite into the cold leg, soft as butter in my mouth, but not melting, inviting me to chew and savor.

"Everything's good," Ernest says, adding salt and pepper to the breast.

The noodles are infused with chicken soup flavor, and they are soft and warm in my mouth. The carrots and celery, soft, too. I taste the crunch and sweetness of the tzimmes.

My taste buds are singing.

The person who sang to me when I was very little was Jampa, my step-grandfather. When he and Gramma lived with us in the mansion on Lake Park Avenue in Chicago, they had a kosher kitchen and we had a traife one. On Gramma's steel sink a whole kosher chicken would lie, its head gone, blood dripping out of its neck into the sink. "*Don't look, kindela,*" Jampa would say before he picked me up. "*Mook?*" he would ask. "*Mook,*" I would say. And he would heat a bottle in water on the gas stove while he danced with me in his arms singing, "*When I was the clock maker at the Tzar's… Tick-tock. Tick-Tock, meina kindela.*" Whenever it was chicken soup time, he would give me my bowl with a cold chicken leg on the side. "*Essen, kindela. Essen.*"

When I was three, we moved away from Jampa, the only person in my family who had ever given me unconditional love. On Passover, we would visit Gramma and Jampa and have chicken soup and I would sit on Jampa's lap. When Jampa was old and blind, and I was grown and married, I would sit my son Ben on his lap, and Jampa's eyes would tear up as he sang, "*Tick. Tock, Benyameen.*"

* * *

I freeze up the rest of the leftover soup to serve at our next family dinner.

RESTORATIONS
2009–2014

I dream of a better tomorrow,
where chickens can cross the road
and not be questioned about their motives.

– Ralph Waldo Emerson

2009

THE STITCHING POST

When I was a pre-schooler, my mother and I would walk to Aunt Marie's apartment on Ashland Avenue. Aunt Marie made me a braid of embroidery floss from which I could withdraw one thread at-a-time without tangling up the others.

Sitting with my mother at Aunt Marie's kitchen table, hearing Mother's clackety-clack knitting needles, listening to the women's chit-chat and being looked after, cheered on, and protected during those rare times when I was the *only* child around are among the happiest of my childhood memories. No older siblings or cousins to tease or taunt me. I think those times when I heard my mother laugh, felt the bond between her and my aunt, and learned a woman's craft in their midst set me on a life-long path of seeking women's friendships and cherishing women's ways of doing.

"For These We Give Thanks," were the words my seven-year old self had stitched with orange embroidery thread on the bottom half of my first sampler. In my mind's eye, I can see the unembroidered cornucopia, printed in blue on the top half of the sampler, waiting for me for another day. But it is gone now, washed away, probably by my sister Jessica as this sampler (and others I had done) came back to me after she died. Mother must have entrusted them to her for safe keeping. *Jessica, did you think the blue-ink was indelible? Jessica...*

Father contributed to my love of sewing, too. In the alley behind our Cornelia Avenue house a junkman's horse pulled a wagon filled with stuff. We could hear the cowbell ring as the cart neared our house. Father made a habit of visiting with the junk man, rummaging through his junk, and treating the horse to a carrot.

When I was nine, Father bought for $1.00 a Singer treadle sewing machine, a black beauty on iron legs. He had learned to sew in the Cavalry on just such a machine and it wasn't long before he had it oiled and raring to go. He made kitchen curtains. He taught Mother how to machine sew but she didn't take to it. Her forte was hand-work.

Father taught me how to thread the machine, wind the bobbin, spin the hand wheel and heel/toe the treadle. At first, I made doll clothes and dresses

143

for my dog Happy but by the time I was thirteen, I was a McCall pattern fashionista. At fifteen, I made my own patterns. My sixteenth birthday present was a White Sewing Machine in a Samsonite case.

A wedding present was a Singer Sewing Machine with nylon gears and a built-in zigzag. On it, I made moss-colored drapes, maternity clothes and baby Ben's stretch-knit outfits. The sewing was not for pleasure. It was from financial necessity. Graduate student stipends did not go far. As soon as I was financially able, I stopped sewing. The Singer has languished for forty-five years in the basement.

I've been told that when one grows older one should take-up again the pleasures of one's childhood because those pleasures will ease the losses and sorrows that inevitably come with age.

So, yes! I want to sew again but I want a new fancy sewing machine that self-threads the needle and has free-motion—the ability to release the "feed-dogs." They look like two rows of canine teeth. They grab the fabric and send it under the needle. With feed-dogs released, the sewer controls the fabric. So, I could draw and write my name in thread. If I wanted to.

* * *

The Stitching Post is in the Bethel Center, just a few minutes away. It is the only nearby sewing store and it is huge occupying the space once occupied by a Big Bear Grocery. Associate Bridget helps me select a Brothers Project Runway brand because it is quiet, light, pretty, self-needle-threading and *Project Runway*. She assures me that with my purchase comes with a lifetime of free lessons, unlimited access to the helpful staff and a year's supply of free needles. She gives me Lesson 1—threading, winding the bobbin, changing feet, and making gathers. She says, "See you next week for Lesson 2."

* * *

GOING OUT OF BUSINESS SALE—EVERYTHING ON SALE

Stores are closing all around me. The auto-supply, video and wedding dress stores gone. Larson's Toys. Friendly's. Book-Bites, Care Uniforms. I am putting my life back together and all around me people are losing their livelihoods.

"Has the global financial crisis hit The Stitching Post?" I ask Bridget.

"Oh, no," Bridget says. "We'll close for a few weeks and then re-open under new management."

"Lesson 2?" I ask.

"Free-motion," Bridget says. "No feed-dogs."

I notice a clutch of employees I haven't seen before. Young men. Wearing ties. *Liquidator staff.* Sociologists have studied liquidator staff. They are trained liars. They lie to regular staff, telling them that they will keep their jobs, so they won't bail out. But the regular staff will be fired.

Other people lying to me or about me or, actually, about anything hits a live nerve. It makes me angry. When I was not yet three, my brother Barrie slid down our banister and slammed into the vase on the newel. It shattered. He said I broke it. Father took Jessica, Barrie and me to the basement, I think so Mother wouldn't know what he had in mind. She did not believe in corporal punishment. She disciplined us by making us sit on a chair and think about what we had done.

Once in the basement, Father gave us an opportunity to confess. I didn't. Jessica didn't. Barrie didn't. Father spanked all three of us saying, "I know I have the right one." It was the only time I was ever spanked. Injustice still smarts. Other people's lying has consequences.

Lying is so wrong. When I was three, I told *my* first lie. A mean girl with red hair and freckles lived next to us. Next to her an African-American family had moved in. I was enamored, the way little children are, with the Boy with milk-chocolate skin and licorice stick hair. He liked me, too. He gave me a marble, a purie that I could see right through and see the world differently than I ever had.

I was walking past the mean girl's house when I slipped on some gravel, scraped my arm and saw my purie roll towards the mean girl's meaner dog. He pulled on his chain. He growled. She came out of the house and called me a "nigger lover." I didn't know what that was, but knew she was bad and was probably saying something bad. Her dog showed his teeth. She pocketed my purie. I went home, crying.

"The mean girl's dog bit me," I told my parents, showing them my scraped arm.

"If that's true," my father said, "that dog will have to be killed." He called the police.

The police came. They took out their guns. The mean girl and her father were in her yard.

"Do you know what 'killed' means?" Father asked me.

"No," I said.

"It means that dog will never ever again be alive. Killed is dead forever."
I cried. I confessed. Father took some money from his pants pocket, gave it to the police and thanked them.

The dog wasn't killed and I have tried to be a truth-teller ever since.

"Don't trust the new staff," I say to Bridget.

"Oh, they're fine," she says.

* * *

RETIREMENT SALE—EVERYTHING 40% OFF

"Can't hardly wait for my next sewing machine lesson," I say to Bridget.
"Fancy stitches!"

"No class today," she says. "But we'll resume classes soon."

* * *

CLOSING TODAY—EVERYTHING 90% OFF

The check-out lane snakes from the half-dozen cash registers at the front of the store to the back of the store, and around the buttons and up again, back and forth, like a giant zigzag stitch. Regular carts are gone. Shoppers have created make-do carts from sewing machine tables.

I usually fear crowds and dislike commotion. I usually relate to the underdog, in this case the staff losing their jobs. I usually hate to wait in lines. I usually hate feeling sand-bagged, manipulated. But instead of fear, dismay, or anger, I am feeling immersed in life. This is the first time since my sister Jessica died that I have felt so alive, so aware of the life around me, all of us shoppers filling our carts with bargains. *OH, how Jessica loved bargains!*

Everyone does grief differently.

I don't recognize myself. I don't know who I am. But I will go with it. I seem to be in sympathy with all these other women who have been lied to by The Stitching Post. I am in a sisterhood. We are all making the best of it in our own ways. Everyone does recuperation differently. I like being enfolded in this women's world.

I hope I am not lying to myself.

"Can I use the bottom shelf of your cart?" a heavy-set woman asks. She's holding bolts of plush fabric to her ample breasts. Her overfull cart is in front of mine.

"Of course," I say.

"My church is making blankets for Appalachian families," she tells me when she deposits her finds.

"It's an ill wind that brings no one good fortune," I murmur.

She begins another foraging trip.

"That's a lot of blue-twill." I overhear the comment.

"For my girl-scout troop." I overhear the response.

Children are running around the store playing hide-and-seek behind the counters and under the cutting-tables. Other children have commandeered carts and are playing dodge-'em. No one is reprimanding the children. Not their parents. Not the staff. Not Liquidation Manager Mike. The store is on its last legs but the children are in free motion.

"Do you do a lot of embroidery?" a woman in purple asks me, pointing to my cart. In it are zillions of packs of fine Italian embroidery thread (at ten-cents a package) and zillions of packs of rayons, cottons, and polys. Every color. Nothing else in my cart but thread.

"I plan to," I answer.

"It's mine!" I hear a woman yell.

"It saw it first," retorts another woman.

"Sorry, it's not for sale," says Manager Mike, whisking away the ceramic horse pulling a cart full of flowers. He has prevented a bargain-basement-type tussle, as I am sure he has been trained to do.

"Look at how much fabric they have." The mother behind me in line has two carts. In one her twin-babies play with button-cards. She points to two Amish women at a check-out. The Amish women are purchasing hundreds of yards of cotton and lots of buttons and threads. They have a check-off list and are paying in cash from different envelopes.

"They're probably buying for their whole community," I say.

"It's supposed to be fifty-cents!" An irate customer shouts at Associate Bridget's check-out lane. Her lane is stopped. "Not the sixty cents you've rung up."

"Give it to her for free," Manager Mike says, letting the line's checking-out continue.

"Do you mind if I cut in front of you?" The twins' mother asks.

"I'm in no hurry," I say.

* * *

At home from The Stitching Post, surprisingly energized and future-oriented, I sort through the potpourri of fabrics I have in plastic boxes in the basement: Mother's lace doilies, Father's dark ties, Jessica's rayon 1940s dresses, my childhood samplers, an army patch of Barrie's, snippets from my sons' layettes, burgundy velvet selvage from my wedding to Ernest.

I want to make something I have never sewn before, something that integrates the old and the new with my new sewing machine and old fabrics and new threads. I want to make something that doesn't privilege machine over hand or hand over machine. Or new over old. Something that respects and celebrates stitchery and fabric differences. Something that depends for its beauty and utility upon the differences.

I will name whatever I end up creating "*Family.*"

2010

BASHI AND LILY

A year ago, I woke up wanting a dog. Last evening, my brother's wife called from Shreveport to say, "We've rescued a dawg, and we've named huh *Happy* aftah Barrie's chial-hood dawg."

But Happy was *not* his dog. She was *my* dog. Father had brought her in a taped-up cardboard box on the Christmas Eve when I was four-and-a-half. No one else guessed that there was a puppy inside that box but I did from the yapping. I named her *Happy* after the dog in Barrie's Elson Reader. Father said she was a rat terrier. I thought he was making that up because she didn't look like the pictures of rats I'd seen. Except for her color.

When I was younger, my family had an old Irish dog, Murphy. Mother told me that when my older sister Jessica was a baby, she wandered out of the yard and started to cross the street. Murphy picked her up by her diapers and brought her back. He was a hero. Much, much later a neighbor boy said Murphy had bitten him. A policeman come to our house. I saw the policeman shoot Murphy dead. In our foyer. I don't know what happened after that.

I was glad that Happy was not an Irish dog. She won't get shot to death.

I dressed Happy in doll clothes and slept with her tucked under my sheet. I saw Father throwing cold-water on her and a neighbor dog because they were "stuck." I saw her give birth in our kitchen to six puppies in a box Father had prepared with one of my blankets. I hid her last puppy to no avail.

Every evening, after Happy ate our leftovers, my parents walked her up the alley to "do her business." She never had dog food, saw a veterinarian or had her teeth brushed. She got fat. She outgrew my dolls' clothes and I made her new, bigger ones that could slip over her head. She never outgrew sleeping with me, keeping my body warm. Imaging her death, brought tears to my eyes. I could cry at will. "Crocodile tears" they are called but they weren't. They came from a deeply imagined sense of loss. Or maybe not imagined but already experienced.

"I bring you sad news," Mother told me on the phone. It was my first month away at college. They were selling the family house and moving to an apartment. "We had to put Happy down."

I didn't cry. Instead, I chain-smoked to choke off my grief.

149

"Barrie has no right to steal my dog's name," I complained to Ernest. "They should just name it *Dawg*."

Now, I wanted one, a young dog, smart, elegant, playful and tiny. A dog I could hide in a pocket so no one could take it away, invisible. I felt as if I had always wanted a dog without realizing it. Ever since Happy's untimely *murder*. My dog!

I began the search. I Googled "small dogs," read dog-breed books and talked to dog owners. I did not want a dog with a high likelihood of deafness, blindness, early dementia, hip dysplasia or any other small-dog trouble. I rejected designer dogs as I didn't want to gamble on how the dog would turn out over time

I settled on the Papillon—the smartest of the toy breeds, the least subject to health problems, and, to my eyes, the most beautiful dog ever—butterfly ears, fox-face, delicate long legs, fine long hair with extra frill on the chest, ears, back of the legs and twirled tail.

But Papillons were a rare breed, hard to find in Ohio, and I for sure wanted one with a *pedigree*.

* * *

"Lynette has a Papillon available in Richmond, Indiana," my friend Pat, a dog trainer, said. "She only breeds AKC pedigreed Papillons. Do you want her phone number?"

When I tell Ernest, he says, "Have you figured out why you want a dog so much?"

"No."

"Guess, we'll have to get one so you can."

I phone Lynette on the speaker-phone.

"Can anything good come out of Richmond?," he asks. Ernest comes from Bloomington, Indiana.

"Lynette? My name is Laurel and I am looking for a Papillon."

"One or two?" Lynette asks.

"Oh, just one," I say.

Ernest has warned that the obligations for a dog are far greater than those for a cat. "Cats can pretty much take care of themselves," he says, "and these High-Society dogs can be pretty demanding."

* * *

Ernest and I drive three hours to Richmond's Petland to see the Papillon. We arrive early and wander up a dog food aisle. A woman in a baseball cap comes in with two Papillons on leashes. They are jumping up and down like Jacks-in-the Box.

"Just look at those two dogs," Ernest exclaims. "Too bad one of them isn't the dog we're here for."

"My God. They are adorable. Look at those fox faces!"

The woman holding the leashes approaches us. "Hi," she says. "I'm Lynette. Are you Laurel?"

"Yes!" I am so glad that I am.

Ernest introduces himself and says, "I was expecting to meet just one dog."

"Well, now we have a choice," I say. I can't take my eyes off the Paps. They are even more beautiful than the ones I've seen in books. And so sprightly. And sweet.

"Bashi and Lily are both ready to go to homes," Lynette says. She hands me a leash attached to Bashi, a black-eared male. She hands Ernest a leash attached to Lily, a brown-eared female. Lily is about half the size of Bashi. "Why not walk them around the store? Then play with them off-leash in the enclosed area."

The dogs walk by our heels turning with us as we snake through the aisles. They heel into the enclosure, and Lily pees and poops.

"They're trained to the Ex-Box," Lynette comments, whatever that is. "Sorry about this," she says as she sprays and mops. "Lily's over-stimulated. She's very sensitive."

Bashi and Lily come from a long line of pedigreed show dogs. Their mother, Greta, is a Grand Champion. Their grandfather lives in Japan and is an *international* Grand Champion. Bashi's name means *little bundle of joy* in Japanese. Four pups were in Greta's litter. The other two are being finished as show-dogs.

"Finished?" I ask, sympathetically.

"Yes," Lynette says.

"Does that mean washed up?"

"No," Lynette laughs. "It means that have the potential to be Grand Champions. They have to win in a lot of shows. Finishing is a very expensive project."

"Why isn't Bashi being finished?" I ask. He cocks his head. "He looks regal to me."

"Bashi was a novice champion in Canada but one of his front feet turns in just a smidgeon so he could never be a Grand Champion in America."

"And sweetheart here?" Ernest holds Lily under her armpits, her feet dangling floor ward. He is looking intently into her eyes.

"Lily has not matured," Lynette says. "It's a shame. She has been in three different homes with three different names and then returned to me each time because she can't be shown or bred. She goes from show-to-show with the other dogs so she spends a lot of time in a kennel in the SUV."

"Poor Lily," I say.

"She's light as a feather," Ernest says.

"She weighs three-pounds—a third the breed's standard."

"She is so gorgeous," I say to Ernest.

"A little darling," he says. She's looking unblinkingly into his eyes. "This princess needs rescuing from the terrible life of a show dog."

Bashi is on the floor by my feet.

"We'll take Lily," I tell Lynette. "She needs a forever home."

Bashi jumps onto my lap and puts his paw on my wrist and his head in the crook of my arm and looks up longingly into my eyes. He is so handsome.

"Laurel?" Ernest gives me a silent talking-to.

"And we'll also adopt Bashi," I say.

* * *

A long three weeks pass before Lynette brings Bashi and Lily to our home. In the meantime, they have been spayed and neutered by the vet she trusts, and we have read their pedigrees. The AKC (American Kennel Club) seal certifies that their three-generations of pedigrees were "compiled from the official Stud Book records." Patrimony matters in the dog world. On their documents, both Lily and Bashi have official names. Lily is Starquest's Party On and Bashi is Starquest's Everybody's Talking. Their lineage includes Grand Champions Queen Bless, Frankly My Dear, Lil Mo Theatrics, and a French rascal named Noveau Lord of Misrule. The silly naming guarantees that no two show dogs will have the same name so there will never be any confusion about who-has-won-what. Same silly naming holds for thoroughbred horses.

Lynette checks the perimeter of our backyard and tells Ernest to fill in some holes in the fence with chicken wire. She takes us to the Weybridge Petland where she picks out kennels, kibble, leashes and other necessities. Dog stuff is shockingly expensive.

Back in our backyard, the Paps run around in increasingly larger circles, chasing each other's tails, yapping. Round and round and round.

"Maybe we're too old for two active dogs," I say.

"Look at how happy they are to be together," Lynette says.

Lynette sets up their kennels in my studio. She attaches two hamster feeding dishes to each kennel. She puts kibble in one dish, water in the other.

"Be sure and keep them hydrated," she says. "And give Lily a dollop of canned food. She needs to gain weight. Call me, anytime. We're family."

* * *

"The dogs have a lot to learn," I say. "They don't want to do their business when they are on their leashes."

"Yeah," Ernest says. "They were apparently taught to pee and poop only on a designated square of concrete."

"But they heel well."

"They haven't been house-broken," Ernest says.

"I like that they won't jump into or out of a car."

"But this nasty hamster feeding thing," Ernest says. "Let's get them a couple of dog bowls."

* * *

Bashi and Lily look at the stainless steel dog bowls and back off. "I think show dogs are trained to only eat in their kennels," I say.

"I'll teach them," Ernest says. He fries up dollops of hamburger. Bashi and Lily sniff. "Come and get it," Ernest says, carrying the delicacy to their new bowls. Bashi cocks his head as if asking, *Is it for me?* Lily gives Ernest a penetrating stare and then dances on her rear legs to get a better sniff. "Dance, Lily," Ernest says, leading her by her nose to the bowl. Bashi stops cocking his head and dances his way to his bowl. "Good Dance!" Ernest says giving Bashi his share.

The hamburger is gone in an instant and they're licking their bowls.

"From now on," I say, "they will have to dance for their suppers!"

* * *

For years, Ernest and I have traveled together all over the world. We even wrote a book about our travels. But of late he has become a home-body while my travel lust has not abated.

"I'm going to sign-on for a Road Scholar cruise across the Atlantic on the Queen Mary," I say to Ernest. We're eating fish and chips al fresco at *our* English pub.

After taking it in, he chokes out, "At least it's not the Titanic."

"I am so glad we have Bashi and Lily because now you'll have companionship when I'm travelling."

"What?" Ernest says, half-choking on a chip. " I thought getting the dogs would keep *you* home." He pauses. "I guess we're in an O.Henry story."

A few more chews and swallows.

"I love them," I finally say, putting Lily on my lap.

"Maybe that's why we have them," Ernest says, handing Bashi a bit of fish.

That night I dream that Bashi and Lily are talking, not knowing that I am overhearing their conversation.

"Which one's life will you save?" Lily asks." "His or hers?"

"Don't know," Bashi replies. "We'll find out when the time comes."

KISSES IN THE DARK

My left foot and calf are swaddled in an Ace Bandage. The nerve block has not worn off, a Donjoy Iceman chills my ankle, and Vicodan circulates in my bloodstream. There is no pain.

Funny to write those four words—"there is no pain"—without my customary introduction: God is Love. I will do it now: *God is Love. There is no pain.* My Christian Science inclined Father taught me this mantra when I was six and had broken my arm falling on the ice because I tried skating like the boys with my hands cupped together behind my back. I trudged through the rest of that Chicago winter with my left arm slung in a piece of torn sheet Father had tied around my neck, the bone healing itself, the bone mending crooked, my first grade teacher the only adult noticing, telling my mother to bring me to a doctor. She did so without my father's consent. Looking at my plaster cast, Father shook his head in anger and disappointment. Ever since then I have associated being incapacitated or sick with the neglect, disapproval, and anger of those who are supposed to love and protect me.

My private room in The Edgemont looks out on an enclosed courtyard with picnic benches, sensible chairs, and a roofed-over smoking lounge. I am lying in bed in my hospital gown in the Rehabilitation Wing, Hallway 100, Room 112. It is good to know where I am. I will be here for the next six weeks.

"Dog-nap," Ernest says, and Bashi and Lily and I settle down on my hospital bed. Each has earned a yellow plastic "I am a Therapy Dog" tag. Ernest settles down with his Kindle, a gift for his seventy-third birthday from our Columbus "blended family." Like so many other "blended" families that arise out of divorces, ours is not a puree. We have chunks that collide, edges that have not worn down. Ernest cried when he read the card signed by all ten of us.

"I'll take the dogs home now," Ernest says. "Okay?"

A man's plaintive voice comes wailing down the corridor every thirty-seconds, "Help Me... Help me."

"Hi, can I come in?" A buxom fortyish woman in a wheelchair is at my door. She's wearing a loose fitting T-shirt, no bra and black shorts.

"Sure."

"I'm Renee. Room 113." Her hair is dark, long, and wavy. Her eyes are hazel, her skin clear. She resembles Jane Russell.

She gives a deep chortle and wheels close to my bed. Her right leg has been amputated above the knee, the left leg below. The right one dangles over her seat. Both stumps are bare.

"You're the one with those dogs, aren't you?" she asks. She seems to be waving her legs, thumping them up and down. She adjusts her catheter between her legs. She extends her neck and retracts it.

"Yes. Bashi and Lily. Papillons. We gave them their forever home."

"Do you think they could visit me?" Renee asks in a husky voice.

Renee wheels herself out.

* * *

"Yes, you can pet them." Ernest's voice down the hallway.

Jingle-jangle.

"Going to see Laurel." Ernest's voice closer to my room.

"Yap."

"Yap."

"Oh! Dogs!" A man's voice.

"You can pet them." Ernest's voice. "Bashi and Lily."

"Thank-you." A smoker's voice.

Jingle-jangle.

"They're friendly." Ernest's voice even closer still.

"Pretty puppies!" A child's voice.

"Yap."

"Yap."

"They're Papillons…Touch their ears."

"Grunt…snort." A woman outside my door.

"Bring them over later, huh? Room 113," a seductive voice. Renee.

The Paps dance into my room, up on their hind-legs, going around in circles, nipping each other's cheeks, yapping their little yaps: "Oh hurrah! Laurel's here!" Ernest puts them on my bed. Bashi stretches out on my chest, a little heating pad. Lily guards my foot.

"Your lunch, Miz Laurel." A West African aide, Vena, puts a tray on my swing-away table. "Your dogs?" Vena backs away.

"They're nice," I say.

"Don't like dogs," she says, backing farther away.

"My dogs don't bite," I say to Vena. "They aren't like African dogs."

"All dogs," she says.

"You can pet these dogs," I say.

"Leave it be," Ernest says, giving me a warning look.

"You don't have to pet them," I say. "But they would like you to."

Vena comes closer and tentatively touches Lily's head. Lily doesn't bat an eyelash. Is this the first time Vena has ever touched a dog?

"She's soft," Vena says.

"Her name is Lily," I say.

"Bye, Lily," Vena says, standing taller. "Call if you need something, Miz Laurel."

* * *

Ring-Ring-Ring.

"Hello."

"Ernest called and told us you are doing fine." My older brother Barrie's voice. As a little boy, he was shy and introverted. To build his confidence, Father introduced him to magic tricks. As a pre-teen, Barrie was on the Kukla, Fran, and Ollie Show. He sawed me in half. White rabbits and gray doves lived peacefully together on our back porch. Now, he's a retired professor of economics and a member of the exclusive Magic Circle in London. He travels the world teaching elite magicians his tricks.

"Are you in pain?" he asks.

"No."

"That's good. You sound tired."

"I am."

"Keep getting well, Honey. I'll call tomorrow."

"Here are you nighttime meds." A nurse is in my room, and hands me three little pills in a plastic cup.

"I'll take the sleeping pill a little later," I say.

"Do as you wish but promise you not sell it."

Ernest turns off my light. Bashi, Lily and Ernest give me good-night kisses in the dark.

* * *

"Yap."

"Yap."

"Is that Lily?" Renee's in my doorway.

"Yap."

"Come here, Lily," Renee says.

Ernest puts Lily on Renee's lap. Her thighs bounce forward. Bashi looks anxiously at me.

"How much would she cost me?" Renee asks pointedly.

Ernest gently takes Lily off Renee's lap.

"Just name your price."

"She's not for sale," I say.

Renee wheels out.

Vena carries in a food tray. "Here's your lunch, Bashi and Lily." She grins at me.

"They love you, Vena," I say, as she puts the main-course plate on the floor.

"*Jesus loves you*," she softly hums, petting Lily, first, and then Bashi.

* * *

"So how long are Papillons expected to live?" I ask my dog-trainer who has come to visit.

"Twelve to fifteen years," she says. "If you walk them and watch their diets."

"I want them to live forever."

"So, where's my dog Lily?" Renee is at the door.

"Vena has her," Ernest says.

"She's not gonna *keep* her, is she? I get first dibs."

"Lily has me as her owner," I say, "and she's planning on living forever."

* * *

Ernest wheels me into the hallway with the Paps on their leashes.

A senile nonogenerian is in a wheelchair by the nurses' station.

"Hi Trevor," Ernest says, placing Lily on Trevor's lap.

"Dog," he says.

"Bye dog," Trevor says as Ernest takes her off.

* * *

"Look at me!" I say, wheeling towards the Paps coming down the hallway. "Oh, Pappidinkers! I love you so!!"

Ernest places Bashi and Lily on my lap. They wash my faces with kisses.

"Well, just look at you!" Ernest says, admiring my wheelchair.

"Dog dog dog." Trevor says.

Ernest puts Lily on Trevor's lap.

"How much would you say a dog like Lily would cost?" Renee asks. She's in the hallway.

"There's a Papillon rescue group," I say.

"But they wouldn't have one like Lily, would they?" Renee says.

"Probably not," Ernest says.

"I'm going to have a big settlement. My lawyer's coming next week." Renee assesses me and then Ernest. "How much?"

"Sorry," says Ernest.

"I wonder if there is a dog protection agency to take abused dogs away— you know, how someone might be reported for abusing Lily—and then, do you think the agency would give Lily to the person who reported the abuse?" Renee thumps her leg.

* * *

Ernest has arrived. It is 9:00 a.m. We pack up my Donjon cooler, DryPro, clothes and books into Edgemont tote-bags. My discharge papers have been filed. I have been deemed of "average intelligence."

"Dogs. This is your last time in my bed, here at Edgemont." I look them square in their eyes. "What do you think of that?"

"Yap-yappity-yap-yap!"

I think that means, *Hip-hip-hooray*.

Vena pets Lily and gives both dogs some cheese.

Ernest wheels me into the hallway.

Renee's door is closed.

* * *

"Lil lee! Lil lee! Lil lee!" Trevor sings.

AUTHENTIC MOVEMENT

OH!
I have toes
and feet and legs.
What a blessing.

I can stand, stretch.
Another blessing.

I can walk,
grow heavy.

Some day
I won't be walking
in this world,

And when that happens,
Let that be a blessing,
Too.

CURTAIN CALL

"There's a serious problem," Vicky emails. "The visual artist for the December show at Tru-Art Gallery has reneged. Time is short—so I am inviting poets to send me no more than five poems. I will mount them as art for the December show. Reception will be as usual from 5–8 on the second Friday."

I look at the list of invited poets—among the city's best. And me, too, because I am a friend of Vicky's. Not on the list are Liz, Dianne, Jennifer and Ellyn. All four have died.

* * *

I love poetry mounted on walls if the poems are short, easily understood, and pretty to look upon because of their shape, calligraphy or colors. I email four of my shaped poems to Vicky.

* * *

"Great to see you, Frank," I say to Frank, our retired radio personality.

"You, too." Frank says.

"Hi, Lois. I love your poems about your mutt Marley."

"Hi, Steve…"

"Hi…"

"Hi…"

"Hi, Vicky."

"Hi, Laurel. Have some veggies. Have some punch."

"Here's one of your poems," Ernest says, pointing to the entrance wall.

A ROUND

to write a poem
any poem   this poem
me again   me again   again me
seventeen   tearstained, defiant   again me
still me   twenty-four   toughened, self reliant
and again and still me   thirty and more   me again
forty   fifty   how many more? again me
hiding   me   seeking
writing a poem
this poem

The next ten or so poems are written by the other poets. They are long and typed in a small font. Unshaped. Several long poems have been printed on scrolls and are locked in a glass case.

"Hey Laurel, here's another one of yours," Ernest is pointing with a carrot stick.

SOURCE

The day the electricity broke down 'cause the wind blew
out the juncture box in our crawl space and the Sears Roe
buck fan stopped and the iron wouldn't heat and the fro
zen orange juice wasn't anymore and what with the dish
washer not going egg dried on the plate and the dog barked
and worried us like a bulky red sweater and we couldn't read
a book or finger a hat band in the dark. What we did was think
of wild violets.

"And over there," he says, "a whole wall to yourself."

HOW THE GREAT STATE OF OHIO'S BLIZZARD BECAME A STATE OF MIND

The first sign of spring
a powder beige moth
flying toward me
wing span a full half inch
or less or more
I didn't look very closely
before I smashed it.

GOODBYE COLUMBUS

gone   gone   gone
gone away   can't play   won't stay
gone to the eye of the hurricane
gone to the emerald sea
gone to get some cherry stones
          & crackerjack & curesall tea
gone to the magic mountain
gone to Camelot
gone   gone   gone
miss Me?

"Not many listeners," I whisper to Ernest.

"Am I the only one?" he asks.

I count twelve people, including Ernest and Vicky. I think about the poetry column that once-upon-a-time ran weekly in the local newspaper, the open-readings at downtown storefronts, the school programs, and the poetry groups and visiting poets who had read for years in bookstores, churches and art galleries. To standing room only crowds.

"Is poetry dead?" I ask.

"You can't republish a single line of poetry without permission from the poet, the publisher, the poet's estate. On top of that having to fork over a small fortune," Ernest says. "Poets' heirs are committing literary homicide."

"Poetry life is different, now," Steve says, overhearing our conversation. "Young people go to poetry slams and rap-meets at coffee shops and bars. They post their poems for free on the internet...read poems for free, there, too. Everybody's a poet. You should check out Bossy Girl's Pinup Joint."

"Should we begin the reading?" Vicky asks.

"Where is everybody?" asks an elderly woman. She has just arrived. Out of breath.

THE FOREVER HOME
2015–

What if all these years are just "A Beginning?"

– Tyrrell A. Richardson

ERRANDS BY CAR

"Car-car," I say. Bashi's and Lily's tails wag. "Ready for your spa day?" I ask. Tails wag faster. I put Lily on the passenger side while Bashi puts himself into a stay position on the driveway. Neither dog ever jumps into a car or runs out any door unless invited to do so. They were trained this way when they were on the show-dog circuit. "Good Boy," I say putting Bashi in the backseat. He promptly assumes down. Lily rides shot-gun.

I drive the seven minutes south on High Street to an old building that houses Shampoodles. Beth is the sole owner. She has a high-pitched sweet voice that my dogs love. She calls them by name, cuddles them and puts them together in a playpen just past the sign-in counter. The Paps can see all the action and Beth's clients can see the Paps. They'll be ready at five o'clock. I have the whole day free for my errands.

As I drive, I notice the changes along High Street, always something different now, faster, sooner, often worser. Cane's Chicken-fingers has filled in the Bull Moose Run, an historical rivulet where the last Wyandotte Indian had made his home. The Melting Pot, once the kids' fondue favorite, is gone, replaced with yet another bank with multiple numbers and initials in its name. Mozart's Bakery and Piano Café has moved into the faux-Mediterranean building that was a cafeteria, then empty, then a Persian rug store and after that a different Persian rug store. Two new Asian cafes abut a massage parlor. That parlor abuts *POLISH! A nail salon.*

Driving north, I take in Graceland, once a horse farm owned by a bookie and a madam. A developer purchased it to create one of the country's first shopping malls. The locally owned Big Bear grocery store anchored the open-air mall, a single-screen movie-theater with popcorn popping in the window brought in families, Isaly's Ice Cream fattened them up, Rogers repaired jewelry, Mr. Watts resoled shoes, Ginny permed hair and Hobbyland sold model airplanes and rockets to my sons. Whatever you needed, you could find in Graceland in locally owned small businesses.

After falling on hard times, Graceland has had a "renaissance." Lining both sides of the mall are national chains—Target, Michaels, Urban Active, Office Max, UPS, Kroger's, Sally's Beauty Supply. Graceland could be

Anywhere, U.S.A. if it weren't that Hobbyland is still there serving sons of sons.

Driving further north, I pass our Veterinarian's new building. *I think we're helping her pay for it.* We had been able to walk our dogs around the corner to her modest clinic. Many of the mainstays of daily living once found by foot in downtown Weybridge—the Home Market, pharmacy, and the Weybridge Hardware Store—are gone. To get food, medicine, hammers and nails, or a Hershey bar, I have to drive. Kroger's. CVS. Ace Hardware. Like it or not, here I come. And, I don't like it. The clerks are less well trained, and it takes so much longer to do my errands than it once did. Not only am I slower, the stores are bigger, the traffic is greater, and I don't like it.

Along Trubury Road, the main northern artery of Weybridge, high density apartments have gone up. Vacant lots have been filled with concrete, asphalt, and narrow strips of colored crushed stones. Office buildings are surrounded by ridiculous dwarf trees. Easements are granted, tax abatements are given. Traffic congestion starts at noon.

But, what is wrong with me? There are some changes in Weybridge that are quite wonderful. Walking distance from my house is a farmer's market. The CVS welcomes our dogs and gives them biscuits. The empty Weybridge Hardware's interior has been redesigned and holds locally owned small businesses: a woman owned letter-press and book-binding store; Henry's upscale bar and café; Anise bakery; and Duo, a to-die-for contemporary furniture store. The Weybridge Inn's restaurant is up and running and has four-stars. Across the street, three new high-end restaurants and two pizza places have opened. Yummy Ice Cream is busier than ever.

Around the corner to the north, the 1915 adjunct high school building has been converted into a facility for performing, visual, and digital arts. I have taken oil painting classes, exhibited quilts and gone to concerts there. Ernest's paintings have won ribbons. BalletMet teaches, playwrights debut plays, song-writers sing. Walking distance from my house a world-class art center.

The Village Square is still here and pops with Sunday night concerts, dog-parades, and art-shows. A "Holiday Tree" is decorated each year. The Vintage Dairy Queen still serves Peanut Buster Parfait. Now, an electronic voice says "wait" when the red light is on. My dogs wait.

How proud I am of my fellow residents. We have fought off national chains from linking-into our downtown. We've deployed every legal and moral means to "Keep Weybridge Beautiful."

* * *

Five O'clock. Bashi and Lily yap their "hellos," and jump up and down as if their legs are on springs. Everyone has admired them and cooed at them. They have had their teeth and ears cleaned, their nails trimmed, their fur bathed, conditioned, and styled. Bashi is sporting a blue-flowery bandana, Lily a pink one. "We're celebrating the spring equinox," Beth says.

* * *

"Hello, Beth?" I am on the phone. "This is Laurel."

"Hi," she says.

"I am so sorry. I forgot to pay you."

"Not to worry…Just put it in the mail when it is convenient."

"Come, Bashi and Lily," I say. "Let's walk to the mail-box and show you off."

"Yap."

"Yap."

"And because you are such beautiful French dogs," Ernest says, "let's go on a dog-walk to Chez Provence and get you a doggie treat."

"Yap!"

Did you say treat?

"Yap!"

MIDNIGHT-SKY BLUE

I complain to Lyn, my trusted horoscope reader, that I am dissatisfied with my spiritual growth. Lyn doesn't even look at her star-chart before she asks me how I feel when I come into my house.

"Awful," I say. "The macadam driveway is crumbling and the lawn's relentless march across it has narrowed it to barely a car's width…and my garage door doesn't want to open. And the brick-steps! They are crumbling under foot. Ernest has mortared them in place, but it's just a stop-gap fix…and there is too much distance between each step…my aging friends can't get in my house…and the house needs painted and I think there's some wood-rot…and in the kitchen the whitish wall covering is peeling off the walls and walls that were once simply white are dimply yellow… and…" Lyn interrupts me and asks about my bedroom. "I hate the color of the walls—lackluster whitish puce."

I phone Karen, the only woman on Creative Paints list of painters.

"I'm just up the street from you as we speak," she says.

A red-haired Karen arrives in her "whites" in her red truck. She urges me to make major changes in my color palette starting in the kitchen. But the kitchen connects to the equally distressed dining room, living room, and hallways, and, looking up the stairwell, I can see the old white-trellis wallpaper of the ante-room and from there the white rose wallpapers of the guest room and co-ordinated striped wallpaper of the upstairs bathroom. Karen suggests we redo it all.

"Doesn't that make sense?" she asks.

"Yes," I say. "Saturated colors—midnight-sky blue, Etruscan golds, summer greens."

"Do you want your bedroom dark or light?" Karen asks.

"I don't know," I say.

Karen and I start with the kitchen, which seemed to have had a life, or death, of its own. Every appliance has stopped working. Or leaked, like the refrigerator and blender. Even the coffee bean grinder ground to a halt.

I become my own contractor.

"Are you fixing to sell it?" the workmen ask me.

"No," I answer. "Definitely not."

I shop the MacSizing of kitchen appliance departments, searching for ones small enough to fit into our Cape Cod house; I sleuth the Tile Store for multi-colored slate backsplashes and the Counter-Top Store for greenish solid-surface counters; I Google for polished nickel cabinet pulls and light switches; and I visit every lighting store in the region looking for modern glass and polished nickel light fixtures, finally found at Lowe's. My days are consumed with conferring with Karen, finding the products, finding the workers to install them, and then monitoring their work. Obsessive-compulsiveness manifests.

The kitchen is finished and so are my contracting days.

"Hire Builders Six," Karen suggests.

For the next months Karen paints and re-arranges my furniture. Builders Six comes. The house gets a concrete driveway, porches, steps, windows, gutters, garage doors, dusty-green colored shake-siding, black dimensional roofing, re-located drains, outdoor lighting, electrical circuit box, recessed lights, shutters, redone wood floors, a library room and a new mortgage with a low interest rate.

Ernest and I have lived in this Revere Street house for over three decades. So very unlike my childhood. Father bought houses that he considered investments to improve and sell for a profit, even after Mother died. One of the last letters I received from him describes a condo he had bought in Key Biscayne, re-decorated himself for "four-hundred dollars" and from which he hoped to turn a "little profit." I had seven different addresses before I turned eleven.

Now, it was as if Ernest and I had moved into a new house without moving. Just like our Papillons, I, too, would have a *forever home*.

Karen and I walk around the outside of the house. "Don't you love it?" she asks.

"I do! If we can only live here for a year, it is worth it."

We walk around the inside. From the basement, Karen has retrieved my carved English Tudor triangle chair and set it in a corner of the dining room. When I was five years old, Father took his three children to an antique store. The cash-poor owner chose to pay Father for his law work with furniture. Each child could choose one piece. I chose the odd, bulky, dark-wood, triangular chair in which I could sit regally, like the princess I really was. I found it gratifying, if surprising, that my parents kept the chair through their myriad house moves until it could have a home with me. That's when I learned that its matching chair is in the Chicago Historical Museum.

174

"Don't you just love it?" Karen asks, admiring her handiwork.

"I do! If we only live here for a day—or an hour!—it's worth it!"

"What's your favorite?"

"All of it...maybe the Midnight-Sky Blue."

"Mine, too." Karen says.

We walk upstairs. Ernest joins us.

Lily and Bashi jump on the bed.

"Dog-nap time?" Ernest asks.

"What about your bedroom?" Karen asks, scratching Bashi behind his ear.

"I still can't decide if I want to go dark or light," I say.

"Maybe you and Ernest want to look at some paint samples? Doesn't that make sense?"

"How about this?" Ernest says, holding a saturated blue-green paint chip. "Mountain Laurel.'"

"Perfect!" I say making a kissing sound. It looks light and dark. When I wake up in the morning, I'll think I'm in a thicket. So will Bashi and Lily.

* * *

"Have a joyful day!" Tina's answering machine says and, I imagine, we will have many of them as she agrees to help me declutter my forever house. Young, energetic, compassionate, a friend I met in an Artist's Way group. We sort through my clothes closet and Tina cleanses it with sage and Tibetan bells. We sort through the linen closet, so full its doors will not close. The horde of unused blankets will bring comfort to others. From my studio, crayons, containers, gift bags, drawing pads and unused stuff will bring joy to preschoolers. Hundreds of books will find new homes. The chaos on my desk-top gets filed or tossed.

"What about all of these?" Tina has come upon a trove of journals on the basement bookshelves.

"Journals where I have published articles," I say. "Those little magazines have poems of mine."

"What about making an archive?"

Writing. My writing. Now, neat, indexed, occupying two-dozen five-inch three-ring binders on my study's shelves. Twelve books, too. So much writing.

* * *

Now, everywhere I look, I can again see gifts that were given to me with love. My entire house is bursting with love tokens. My body feels the vibrations. In my study, The Women Prophets poster, a gift from Linda, a cartoon from my friend Ellyn, hand-made paper from Nan, photos of my Memoir Writing group, the photo taken by Mr. Feenly of the Chicago Tribune at Dolly's Sixteenth Birthday party—me seven, center stage, bursting with energy—a Certificate of Merit presented to my sister Jessica for her work with developmentally delayed children, on my desk the Lalique St. Francis, a gift from my sister to my brother to me, and a turquoise bowl from my granddaughter Shana, and under the bowl, *Learning Landscapes*, a book about poetry as a research tool, dedicated to me by its editors, the desk, itself, crafted by my son Josh, and the computer updated by my grandson, Akiva. On the windowsill, a 1971 Florida post-card from my father to my son Ben. Out my picture-window, I see a circus of birds and squirrels, invited to our yard by a food buffet and heated bird-bath, maintained by Ernest.

Love all around...

On my bulletin board a push-pin secures the photo of my mother in her black bathing suit, arms stretched up fixing her long black hair. Next to her is the law-school graduation photo of my father. Mother looks at home, here and now, amongst the photos of her family—one taken of her three children ten years ago, when we were all well and alive. Just me, now. On the bulletin-board hand-written letters to me from Jessica and Barrie and a crumpled old streetcar map of Chicago. I can imagine Mother saying, "Tyrrell, you're right...*Location, location, location.*"

COME WALK WITH ME, AGAIN

Lily and Bashi are ready. Each one sports a black harness, a short leash, and a Martindale collar with jingle-jangle metal tags and their yellow plastic "I am a Therapy Dog" tag. I am ready, too, wearing a flowery muumuu I had bought in Hawaii umpteen years ago. My feet are secure in funky socks and orthopedic Mary-Janes. We head out the side-door, down the new concrete steps onto the new cement driveway.

Lily stops and gives me an exasperated look. "Don't you know by now? I don't want to go west on Revere Street, I want to go south on Concord Street. That's where all the excitement is."

Two years ago, the house next door to the east was purchased by a couple who had grown up in Weybridge and wanted their two young girls to do the same. Jim's a carpenter, Mary's a decorator.

"Hi Chrissie," I say to their five-year old. She's in a two-piece bathing suit sans shoes. She hugs Lily.

"Can I pet Bashi?" asks her three-year old sister, Maddie, wearing a flowery one-piecer. She gently touches my muumuu. "I like your style," she says.

"We're going to the pool," Chrissie tells me.

"Oh how wonderful," I say.

"Are you old enough to be in the deep water?" Maddie asks me.

"*Barkity-barkity-barkity.*"

Bailey, a curly haired rescued dog, runs out their side-door.

He has a perpetual smile on his muzzle. He sniffs Bashi's rear-end and collides with me.

"Paws off, Bailey," I say.

"*Barkity-barkity-barkity.*"

"Sorry, 'bout that," Jim says, corralling Bailey back into the house. "We're going to have to get an invisible fence."

"Can Bashi go to the pool?" Maddie asks. She's petting his ears.

"Thanks for asking," I say. "But he needs to get his walk."

"C'mon girls," Jim says. "Get in the truck."

"Hi." A neighbor, Esther, joins us.

"Hi, Miss Esther," Crissie says.

"Hi, Esther," I say.

"How come you can call her *just* Esther?" Maddie asks me.

"Miss Laurel is a grown-up," Jim explains.

Esther moved into the house behind me, the one where the old man who had poisoned my cat, Blue, once lived. Esther rescues dogs and has a dog-sitting business. She has a large, fenced-in yard with features of interest to dogs like trees, a shallow pond, bushes and barking access to the street and four adjacent backyards. Lily and Bashi often stay for a few hours when Ernest and I are both gone. Sometimes they have overnights.

"How's Major doing?" I ask. Major is her latest rescued dog. He's a big old guy with arthritis and hip dysplasia. Sometimes, I walk him with my Paps. I feel empowered holding his leash.

"The acupuncture's helping," Esther says. "Oh, and I have something for you." Esther hands me a freshly breaded and baked challah bread. "Also, I am having a play-date for small dogs on Tuesday at 10:30."

"We'll come," I say. "I'll bring napkins." I have paper napkins of French Bulldogs in party hats at the Eiffel Tower.

"You're *meshuganah*," she says.

"You're crazy, too!" I say.

* * *

"Hi, Tony." Tony calls himself a "washed-up poet." He is zapping his weeds with weed-killer. He lives on the corner of Concord and Putnam.

"Where's Ernest?" Tony asks.

"Oh, he decided to sit this chapter out," I say.

"Sitting on that desk-chair I put out for the pickers?"

"Absolutely!"

* * *

Jeannette and her wife Rachel are sitting on their brightly painted Adirondack chairs. I know these women from the university. Their dog Riley, a Golden Retriever, is stretched out on the grass. He's a therapy dog for the funeral home on High Street. My dogs and Riley are uninterested in one another. I don't know why.

* * *

"Woof! Woof! Woof!" Pulling on her twelve-year old handler is the Pomeranian, Cutesy. She is my dogs' BDF, Best Dog Friend. The Paps *yap-yap* their hellos and the three meet in the middle of Putnam Street, sniffing and circling and sniffing again. And then they are done with each other. I really don't get how my dogs do friendship. It is not the sniffing part that puzzles me, it's how soon they are finished being with each other. When I see my friends or talk to them on the phone, hours might pass and even then I might want more time. Dogs seem able to get what they need when they need it and move on.

* * *

"What's this?" I ask the dogs. They are busy sniffing a pile of branches tied-up on a lawn.

"Hi," a young man says. "I'm Patrick."

"Hi, Patrick." I introduce myself and the dogs.

"Hi," a young woman pushing a baby-stroller joins us. "I'm Natasha. This is Vlad. He's two."

Bashi and Lily are prancing about. Nothing pleases them more than a toddler in a stroller.

"Pup-py! Pup-py!" chants Vlad. He reaches for Lily. She puts her paws on his leg. Bashi rubs against the stroller and puts a paw on Vlad's shoe.

"Do you mind if I take a picture?" Patrick asks.

"Of course not, snap away."

* * *

Marge is walking slowly with her walker. After her husband died, she moved in with her son's family.

"How's it going, Marge?" I ask.

"It's hard," she says. "My daughter-in-law has such different ideas about how to run a house…what to cook…how children should behave…I talk to my son about it, but he doesn't hear me.'

"Three generation families are hard," I say. "I lived in one when I was little."

"Well, I'm going to do something about it," Marge says. "I'm going to have all my women neighbor friends for tea one day a month. You'll come won't you?"

"I look forward to it," I say.

* * *

Mac is detailing a camouflaged Humvee on his driveway. Two high-end BMW's sit in his driveway, waiting.

"Was that Humvee in Afghanistan?" I ask.

"Or Iraq." He calls me over and points to a trash can full of sand. "Genuine Desert souvenirs," he says.

* * *

The Trent's house is still empty. They moved after their son's addiction to heroin blossomed into burglary.

* * *

"GraceAnn, how's your ankle?" GraceAnn is from Ghana and line dance has been her passion. Now knee replacement has side-lined her. She has a newly adopted brown puppy, Bella. Bella strains on her leash to reach the Paps. Bashi strains on his. Lily refuses to budge. Bella is going to have to come to her. When she does, Lily goes into a play-bow, front legs down, bottom wiggling in the air. She has the Pap's signature openmouthed smile and slaps her forepaws on the grass in front of Bella.

"Will she hurt Bella?" GraceAnn reaches to pick up her puppy.

"Nah," I say. "She's socializing her." Lily pant-laughs and circles around Bella in figure eights. She slaps the grass again. Bella play-bows. "Look at how quickly Bella's learning," I say.

"Next you know, she'll be line dancing," says GraceAnn.

* * *

Gerry and her dog, Monet, are in Gerry's car. Monet's shaggy white head is sticking out the rear window. Gerry's a member of the Weybridge Area

Art League of which Ernest had been president. Bashi is preparing to bark. "Quiet! Bashi." I give him a treat. "Good dog." *He* thinks that's one of his names.

"I saw your *Family* quilt at the High Road Gallery show," Gerry says. "Congrats on winning an honorable mention."

"Pretty nice, huh," I say.

* * *

Han and his wife Xiao are carrying buckets of water and pouring them on their grass. They don't use hoses for watering. I would ask them why but they are not English speakers. I wave. They bow. I tell Lily and Bashi to bow, too. They bend their front legs and lower their heads. Han and Xiao laugh.

* * *

Many of the houses have turned over since we moved here. Many of them in the past few years, almost all now inhabited by young families with dogs. New driveways, siding, windows. Raised roofs. The dogs sniff around a newly arrived sign in a front-yard: Builders Six.

Swings are in front-yards, one is made from a skate-board, another is plastic, a third looks like a flying saucer on chains, and a fourth is a suspended wooden-seat like the one suspended from the century old Elm tree in my back yard, the swing that caught my memories and convinced me to buy my Revere Street house. That swing is gone, the elm long since felled.

A clutch of boys and girls are playing from lawn to lawn with Frisbees. A terrier joins them. A bevy of boys on bikes and skate-boards whiz past. Lily cowers. Bashi yaps at them. *"Don't you dare come near My Laurel and My Lily."*

* * *

Clona, the personal helper for Mr. and Mrs. Rainey for almost five years, sees us and comes out to greet the Paps and me. Mr. Rainey died a few months ago at ninety. He had a funeral with full military honors.

"How's that Yorkie-Prince of yours?" I ask.

"Not good," she says. "He has leukemia. The vet put him on prednisone but we'll probably have to put him down."

"I am so sorry, Clona."

Clona's grief is palpable. "And my mother died on Thursday."

"OH!" I say."There is nothing like losing a mother."

"My sisters and me gave her the last dose…morphine…under her tongue…I feel like I killed her."

"No, you didn't," I say, and then stop myself and acknowledge her feelings. "So sorry, Clona. "

"My sisters are angry. They say God is a mean God."

"And you?"

"I caint talk to my sisters."

"Everyone grieves differently," I say. "I'm so sorry."

"The hospice nurse gave me book about how people die. So, I read it. Dying doesn't just happen…she was getting there all by herself…we didn't kill her."

"Sounds like a good book," I say. "My brother just died…"

"Very short book…maybe five pages…I'll bring it on Wednesday and you can borrow it." She pets Bashi. "Well, I'd better go in and give Mrs. Rainey her dinner."

* * *

"What's this?" I ask the Paps. They have discovered a new neighborhood feature, a Little Lending Library, a sweet triangular shaped house-like thing with a tin roof. I browse.

* * *

Rrrrr. Rrrrr. "Big noise!" I say to Bashi. "Sorry, I don't have your thunder shirt with me." The Ohio State University is succeeding in turning what was once a small airport for training Air Force ROTC into what they are dubbing the "Corporate Gateway." They are doubling the landing strip to accept commercial jets, lowering flight paths and adding more approaches. The new paths fly over the Weybridge's schools, religious centers, libraries, historic buildings, daycare centers, hospital, commercial buildings, recreation centers, and all the houses in the township.

Weybridge citizens have fought this development for two decades, but we have lost. We are like the Wyandot Tribe that once resided here. Neither we nor they can win against deep pockets.

* * *

Three SUV's are parked in front of my favorite flat-roofed house. Carrying boxes are two sets of parents of a new couple moving in today. Jackson, a lumbering Labradoodle, commands the lawn with a waging tail. He play-bows to Lily, who snubs him. She prefers girl dogs.

"My daughter's due in December," says a grandfather-to-be.

"They are so happy to have found a home here in Weybridge" says the other grandfather-to-be." Weybridge is the second most desirable zip-code in the whole nation, according to a survey of real estate brokers.

"Hi," a pregnant woman comes out carrying a laptop. "I'm Aisha."

"Welcome!" I say. "Glad you're here. We're back-yard neighbors."

* * *

And I am glad. What had once been a developer's name for my neighborhood—Selden Village—has transformed into an actual model village alive with children and pets and people who know each other. We even have a Facebook page. Outside our boundaries the world might be changing into look-alike strip malls and Moscow-Arms style apartment buildings that disencourage engagement, but here, inside Selden Village, older residents and newcomers are creating and celebrating diversity in community.

* * *

"C'mon, Lily," I say. She's pulling back on her leash. "We're going to walk up Revere Street just because I want to. You may be the dominant dog, but you are not in charge of me."

Reluctantly, Lily heels alongside Bashi. But once she realizes that we are not heading toward Lexington Boulevard, the little valley and the Secret Wilderness but that we really are heading for home, there is no holding her back. We don't chase after the doe and her two fawns nibbling on grass. We note the fox and her kits near Joe's water-feature, but we do not stop. We race past Lucky and Chance, the rescued beagles, we ignore Tinkerbelle, Rhonda and Dale out jogging, Fido V, and our next-door neighbor Martha tending her garden and Bob climbing a ladder by his driveway and their son, Robert, now a grown man with full mustache, securing the ladder.

"How'd this get here?" I ask the dogs. A rear-view car mirror is on the pavement no more than twenty feet from our driveway. "Don't know? I guess we'll have to ask Ernest about it."

We reach our home. I look around at the century old trees, the mid-summer splash of colors on flower-beds, and the blue sky with wisps of clouds. Our black cat Asia greets us at the front door stoop, stretches and mews.

"You know, Paps," I say to Bashi and Lily so that they will know, in case they don't, "it doesn't get any better than this. It may get just as good, but it doesn't get any better."

AFTERWORD

HERE. NOW.

Now let the primitive binary of this or that,
Black or white,
Here melt, thaw, resolve itself into a dew
Into the vastness.

We push our barrows of broken stone
To the Construction Site—
Saint Peter's, Salisbury, Stonehenge,
Los Alamos
The Globe
The Great Wheel of Space and Time.

We are Here.
Now.

Ernest Lockridge

APPRECIATION

This book was once twice this size. Reaching this size depended on the scrupulously attentive and tender critique of my husband, Ernest Lockridge. He read and re-read and red-lined different chapters in this manuscript covering thirty-five years of change more times than either of us care to remember. And, he has lived through those thirty-five years with me, calming my anxieties and holding both my hands. He generously allowed me to use his poem, "Here. Now.," as the Afterword for this book. No matter how much I try, I can't thank him enough. "It's nothing," he says. So, I thank him again and show him this paragraph. And he says, "How nice of you."

For fifteen years, Memoir Writing group—Linda Thompson, Linda Royalty, Deanne Witiak, Diana Newman, Beverly Davis, Erica Scurr and the late Nancy Lee—has provided gentle critiques and unremitting support for me and this project. They are irreplaceable. I love them all.

My friend and colleague, Julie White (Victoria Institute, Melbourne) has not only supported this project through our Skype conversations and pre-conference retreats she has honored me with writing the book, *Permission: The International Interdisciplinary Impact of Laurel Richardson's Work* (Sense 2016). The idea of *Permission* and Julie's engagement with its fifty contributors has been a sustaining force for me.

For the past year, the writing group, Scriveners, has given me excellent feedback and support. I thank Barb Fiorini, Nancy McDonald-Kenworthy, Thom Pegan and Patricia Snyder.

Personal support from special friends and colleagues—Ellyn Geller, Carla Corroto, Nan Johnson, Patricia Lynch, Carolyn Ellis, Elaine Ebert, Susan Knox, and Norman Denzin has made such a difference.

Editor Patricia Leavy has been a joy to work with. She has done more than I could ever have imagined. Her staff, Shalen Lowell, and Jolanda Karada (Sense Publishers) have worked so well and quickly to bring this book to fruition. Some wonderful and generous people have written blurbs for this book. Peter de Liefde of Sense Publishers is a true visionary. I thank all of them.

My sons, Ben Walum and Josh Walum, are precious resources as are Tami Walum, Akiva Walum, Shana West, Melissa Martin and Kenneth Martin. Ernest's children and grandchildren and our weekly blended family dinners bring festivity into my life. My sister, Jessica Richardson, encouraged me to "do what you want." My brother, Barrie Richardson, gave me the idea for the sub-title of this book. "It's an Americana book," he said the last time I saw him, three weeks before his death. My parents, Rose Foreman Richardson and Tyrrell A. Richardson gave me the tools and desire to learn about people's lives, including my own.

And, of course, without my Papillons Bashi and Lily's overwhelming desire for my company, I would have had this book done sooner, but with a less joyful conclusion.

APPENDIX A:
WHY *SEVEN* MINUTES?

Early readers of this book asked, "Why *seven* minutes from home?" My response was that seven minutes is all the farther from home that I liked to go—by foot, bike, bus or car. Within seven minutes of my home there is shopping, restaurants, theaters, doctors, gym, dog park and libraries. Most of my friends live nearby. All of my literary and art groups meet nearby. If something is planned outside my seven minute preference, I feel annoyed. Columbus is a geographic giant. Rush hour starts before 4:00. I often choose to bypass events that are "too far" from my home. Takes too much time.

But my answer, I realized, side-stepped the point of the question: Why *seven* minutes? Why not eight? Six? Ten?

I really didn't know. But I wondered if I could find out *why*.

I google "number seven." Five billion plus entries show up. Possibly, my subconscious choice of 7 had been over-determined.

* * *

I grew up believing the world had seven seas, seven continents and Seven Wonders. Seven colors were in the rainbow, seven notes in the diatonic musical scale, and seven holes in my head.

In mythology, I learned that Atlas had seven daughters whose affairs with gods helped populate the heavens. Poor Atlas, while forced to carry the heavy weight of heaven on his shoulders, Orion found an opportunity to pursue the daughters. Zeus, taking pity on Atlas, transformed the daughters into a seven star configuration, the Pleiades. Orion still pursues them in the night sky. Pleiades is the first constellation-story I learned. A weird boy, chased after me, caught me and threw me into a huge cement-sided sandbox, insisting that he was Orion and that I had come from the Pleiades. I had fifteen stitches on my right leg. I still have the scar. We were seven year olds.

In Christianity, there are many sevens—deadly sins, gifts from God, and sacraments. In Revelations, the Seventh Angel will blow the seventh trumpet seven times and a lamb will break open the seven seals to reveal the mystery of God.

In New Age spirituality, one's number (based on one's name and/or birth date) signifies one's life path. Seven signifies a life path of introspection, analysis and spirituality. (That sounds like my path.)

In the mystical Jewish tradition of Kabbalah, which I find fascinating, seven is the spiritual number. God created the world in *seven* days. On the seventh day, it isn't that God rested; rather, God added a spiritual dimension to the creation. God blessed it. The world was made whole and complete on that Sabbath (seventh) day. Our time designations follow the sun, the moon, and the seasons, except say Kabbalists, for the "God-created and human-adopted" seven-day week. They also say that there are not *six* directions— east, west, north, south, above, below—but *seven*, the seventh being the middle, the place where you are.

And, of course, there is the idea in the West that 7 is a lucky number. Seven does actually have the greatest probability of coming up during a roll of two six-sided dice. Slot machines pay-off with triple sevens, 777.

There seems to be no end to 7 in our environment, history and imagination: the seven hills of Rome; seven liberal arts; Saptarishi in Ancient India; 7–11 convenience stores; 7 Up soda pop; James Bond's 007; Snow white and the Seven Dwarfs; seven year itch; Star Trek's Gary Seven; Killer7 video game; seven novels in the Harry Potter series; manga series, *nana* (seven in Japanese); David Bowie's *Seven;* the maximum number of playoff games in NHL, MLB, and NBA; George Carlin's "Seven Words You Can Never Say on Television;" 7 chakras; Islam's seven hells in hell; seventh son of seventh son; +7 calling code for Russia; and hundreds—maybe seven hundred-thousands—of other associations.

Hmm. Books. *Seven Habits of Highly Effective People; Seven Pillars of Wisdom; The Magnificent Seven; The Secret Seven: The Seven Dials Mystery; House of Seven Gables; Seven Minutes from Home: An American Daughter's Story.*

* * *

Psychologists propose there is a neurological basis for our preference for 7. Our short term memories do best if we organize our thoughts or chores in units of seven. Most of us can remember seven digits read to us, but not eight. Neurologists have explained why: our hippocampus does best when its dendrites (the branches that get stimulated) number seven. We like 7 because that's what our brains are best able to store.

Plus, I really like 7 because it is the only single digit that has two syllables. Plus, it rhymes with heaven. Plus, would you want to read about a secret agent named 008?

Corporations build drugstores, convenience stores and service stations seven minutes apart for those travelling by car. This is not an accident.

So, *Why NOT seven minutes?*

* * *

In all my thinking and reading about 7, though, I realize that I have overlooked the deeply embodied basis of my preference for traveling only seven minutes from home in my everyday life. Growing up I could walk everywhere within seven minutes—school, park, library, stores, friends' houses. I was in the middle of everywhere I wanted to go. As my father would say, "What matters is location, location, location."

* * *

And you know what else? I was a very very very happy seven-year old.

APPENDIX B:
FURTHER ENGAGEMENT

DISCUSSION QUESTIONS

1. In *Seven Minutes from Home,* the author demonstrates the interconnection between our individual biographies and socio-historical contexts. Select one chapter and discuss how the author makes those connections. What do we learn about the larger world when we see it through her personal experiences?
2. Place is a prominent theme in *Seven Minutes from Home.* Place has a profound impact on each of our lives. What kind of neighborhood (s) have you grown up in? How has growing up in the same neighborhood or moving to new ones impacted your life? Consider the people, social climate, schools, transportation, work-opportunities, community and sense of safety (or danger) that affected you and your family.
3. Status characteristics such as race, gender, class and sexuality, and the interaction between them, influence our life experiences and opportunities. Select two experiences where gender has impacted the author's life. What do those experiences tell us about gender? Have you had similar experiences?
4. Choose another status characteristic such as social class, education or ethnicity. How has the interaction of that status with gender impacted your life?
5. Family is one of the central themes in the book – the author's mixed family of origin, her first marriage, her current blended family, and the families that she writes about. How has the author conveyed *differences* in family structures? Does her writing work to *normalize* these differences, and if so, how? Do you belong to one, or more, of these family structures? How do you negotiate your life in different kinds of families?
6. The author asserts that lying is always wrong and has unexpected consequences. What do you think children should be taught about lying? How should they be socialized in this moral arena? Did your family, peer-group and/or community define "lying" in the same way? Do you have to negotiate between worlds? If so, what have been the consequences for your sense of identity?

7. What kind of truth is the author telling in this book? Emotional? Relational? Experiential? Personal? Choose one of the chapters and explain why you think it is an authentic account, or why you think it is not.

8. Pets play a major role in many American homes. In 2010, the author adopts two dogs. How have they changed how she interacts with her world? If you have/had a pet, has it changed your interactions with other people? Consider ways in which American society anthropomorphizes pets and expends big-bucks on them. What's going on here? Why?

9. Re-read "Memorial Day Parade." What different discourses about peace/war does the author present? Or there other discourses, or amplification of discourses, you think could/should be added?

10. How do you understand the title and subtitle of the book? Do they describe the book to you? In what way(s) do you see yourself, or not see yourself, as an American daughter or son?

11. In what particular ways is this book *not* a son's story?

12. Earlier waves of feminism focused on women's rights to choose their own destinies. How has the author illustrated, or not, that wave of feminism. Third wave feminism focuses on expanding feminist ideals to all people and their relationships to the planet, including animals. How has the author embraced, or not, this third wave feminism?

13. An author must make choices about what to include in an autoethnography. Do you think the author made choices that empowered or disempowered women of different educational and economic levels?

14. How does the author handle female friendships? As a reader, do you assume the author's friends are heterosexual? Why, or why not?

15. Women and beauty is a continuing story in American culture and one raised in *Seven Minutes from Home.* How do you think women should deal with the "beauty" and "anti-aging" discourses in American culture? Do you see any contradictions, between make-up, tattoos, dieting and spandex undergarments with women's goals for equality? What about cosmetic surgery? Do you think "beautification" lines should be drawn? Are there different expectations for men? Are those changing?

RESEARCH PROJECTS

1. Children and trauma is a recurring theme in the book. Locate pop culture examples of children being traumatized. Does race, gender, class, ethnicity, "looks" or nationality affect how pop-culture treats child-trauma?

2. Interview a relative, friend, neighbor or teacher who is from a different generation than you about 9/11 or some other memorable day. Ask questions that help the interviewee to locate their personal experience within the public event. Interview another person of that same generation but of a different gender, class, race or ethnicity. Have your interviewees given different accounts? What do you make of those differences?

3. Make a map of the world within seven minutes from your current home or one where you grew-up. What landmarks are important to you? Why? Is your map an architectural one? Interactional, e.g. people you know and places you go? Critical theoretical, e.g. poverty, lack of diversity in people, property and stores? Or something different?

4. Try superimposing architectural, social-interactional and socio-cultural maps upon each other. Does the visual interplay help you (or not) understand the relationship between the personal and the public? Does it stimulate memories? Insights?

5. Dogs and cats are more common in American people's homes than children. Researchers from different disciplines study the "human and non-human species" connection. Google about this. Share what you find out.

6. Go to a pet-store, dog show, dog shelter or dog park. Observe the interactions between the people and the pets. Take field-notes, i.e. record what you see without judgment. Any hunches? For example, are different human characteristics imputed to dogs based on the dog's sex, size, or rarity? Go back to your observation site. Observe again. Go to another dog site. Observe. Go to a different site. Keep taking notes. Keep getting hunches. (Be careful, you might find yourself writing a thesis. Or adopting a dog.)

7. Consider one of the heavily populated chapters such as "Come Walk with Me, Again," "Secret Recipe," "New Year's Eve" or "The Stitching Post." Create an ethnodrama (a dramatic rendition) based on that chapter. Cast it and find an audience!

8. What is it like to be physically challenged, infirm, or aging? In *Seven Minutes from Home* the author explores how the built environment might not accommodate those with special needs, even when those needs are minor. If you are able, go grocery shopping in a motorized cart that many stores now provide. Pay attention (take field notes) on how people respond to you. Do you become invisible? Do you become a "child"? Are people helpful or do you feel you are in the way? If you can't use the cart, but are able, walk with a cane or a walker. Or, find other ways

to project a physical challenge. If you already have a physical challenge, you can project a different one or write about your experience (s) in an unaccommodating world.

9. The author writes about unorthodox families," e.g. Jewish/Gentile, Somalian/White American, same-sex, blended, tri-generational, cross-ethnicity and so on. Interview a person who grew up in an unusual family structure about how the family negotiated everyday activities, such as food, bed-times, schooling, shopping and health. What new have you learned about the variety and permeability of cultures?

10. *Seven Minutes from Home* covers a thirty-five year (1980–2015) period in the United States. The author describes changes in her body, the built environment, and the socio-cultural one. Choose a long-running magazine (e.g. *Seventeen, Vogue, O (Oprah) Time* or another of your choosing). Sample issues from those 35 years, perhaps one for every five or seven years. Choose a theme or question, e.g., representation of women of color in ads, articles about losing weight, heterosexual relationship problems, lesbian relationships, beauty etc. How has the coverage changed, or not changed, over the 35 years? (If you are unable to locate the earlier versions of the magazines, sample another cultural product, e.g. TV. shows, movies, catalogues, Pulitzer Prize winners, Caldecott winners, classroom math books, etc.) The idea of this project is to consider social change as presented (or reflected) in media over a defined historical time and place. (Perhaps choose a magazine or media format that is unfamiliar to you but that you have been curious about.)

11. Consider the author's poetry in *Seven Minutes from Home.* How are women presented? Choose a contemporary poet (or song lyricist) and do a content analysis of how women are presented. Perhaps contrast a famous male with a famous female lyricist or poet. In what ways are they similar? Different? How do you explain the similarities? Differences?

CREATIVE WRITING

1. Choose a scene in *Seven Minutes from Home* that the author has written as dialogue. Rewrite that scene as exposition. Now, choose a scene that the author has written as exposition and re-write it as dialogue. What have you gained, or lost, by those re-writings?

2. Choose a passage of description and analyze its function in the chapter. How does it add or detract from the theme and significance of the narrative?
3. Choose one of the "minor" persons in one of the book's scenes. Re-write that scene from the point of view of that person.
4. Which person would you like to know more about? Write that person's back-story and put that person in a scene.
5. A new literary genre is called the "hybrid genre." It allows the author to include poetry, memoir, history, ethnography and other forms of writing in one book. *Seven Minutes from Home* is an example of the hybrid genre. Choose a vignette from your life and write it in different ways, such as a poem or dialogue. Remember what you have is "material" and material can be shaped and re-shaped. You can write a hybrid.
6. After reading "Appendix A: Why Seven Minutes?" write a different list of *why* seven minutes. Introduce other cultural and generational ideas. Or, reject "seven" and write about another number?
7. Humor plays a big part in *Seven Minutes from Home.* Why? Can you rewrite something you have written in a serious mode to a humorous one?
8. In the book, the author's husband, Ernest, appears frequently as a catalyst, a fellow-traveler and a conversationalist. The author wants the reader to like Ernest as much as she does and she wants the reader to like their relationship. What writing strategies has she used? What writing strategies might you use to write about your go-to person? Write a scene.
9. Several of the chapters are especially cinematic, such as "The Stitching Post" and "Memorial Day Parade." Write a screen play for one of the chapters that appeals to you cinematically.
10. Locate the poems in the book. Decide if they add or subtract from the narrative and in what ways.
11. In Seven Minutes from Home, the author has changed the identities of persons and places, with the exception of her immediate family. She has tried to treat the people respectfully. This has required a number of drafts. So, as a draft-writing exercise Take a real-life situation about which you feel angry or hurt. First, just write it up. Second, change all the identifiers of the persons and places. Third, make everyone have at least one redeeming feature. What have you discovered?

12. There are nine speakers in the chapter, "New Year's Eve." How has the author managed, or not managed, to differentiate the speakers? How might you have done it?

13. Write a story of your own about your life within seven minutes from home. Consider how your personal experiences are a catalyst to talk about larger environments. If you can't think of a topic to get started, try one of the following:

    a. Your first day in elementary, middle or high school.
    b. Your first college class.
    c. Your first driver's test.
    d. Your first pop-concert.
    e. Your first "none of the above" test-question frustration.

ABOUT THE AUTHOR

Laurel Richardson is Professor Emeritus of Sociology at The Ohio State University where she was also an Adjunct Professor of Women's Studies and a Distinguished Adjunct Professor of Cultural Studies. She is an internationally renowned researcher in qualitative methods and arts-based research. She has pioneered social science writing as poetic representation, ethnodrama, memoir, layered texts and autoethnography. Her writing models ways in which the private and the public intersect.

She has received multiple awards for her teaching, mentoring, and service for women and minorities and has been honored in sociology, gender, and creative writing. *Permission: The International Interdisciplinary Impact of Laurel Richardson's Work* includes over fifty tributes to her. The International Congress of Qualitative Inquiry honored her with the Lifetime Achievement Award for "dedications and contributions to qualitative research, teaching and practice."

Richardson's work reflects her ethical quest: How can we write to empower others? She has written over two hundred articles and ten books. Her books on gender, ableism and writing include: *The Dynamics of Sex and Gender* (the first text in the field), *Feminist Frontiers* (co-edited anthology, now in its seventh edition), *The New Other Woman* (translated into seven languages), *Gender and University Teaching* (co-authored), *Writing Strategies: Reaching Diverse Audiences* (a first in its field), *Travels with Ernest: Crossing the Literary-Ethnographic Divide* (co-authored, first in its field), *Fields of Play: Constructing an Academic Life* (C.H. Cooley Award Winner), *Last Writes: A Daybook for a Dying Friend, and After a Fall: A Sociomedical Sojourn* (Honorable Mention/Best Books ICQI).

In addition to her academic accolades, Laurel Richardson has received awards for her poetry, photography, and fiber art. She is grateful for all the good things in her life, including her friends, colleagues, spouse, family and her four four-footed creatures.

Made in the USA
Middletown, DE
23 June 2016